By Mark A. Robertson and James A. Calloway

Winning Alternatives to the Billable Hour

STRATEGIES THAT WORK

THIRD EDITION

formerly *Win-Win Billing Strategies* edited by Richard C. Reed

LAW PRACTICE MANAGEMENT SECTION

MARKETING • MANAGEMENT • TECHNOLOGY • FINANCE

Commitment to Quality: The Law Practice Management Section is committed to quality in our publications. Our authors are experienced practitioners in their fields. Prior to publication, the contents of all our books are rigorously reviewed by experts to ensure the highest quality product and presentation. Because we are committed to serving our readers' needs, we welcome your feedback on how we can improve future editions of this book.

Cover design by Jim Colao.

Form Fee Agreement reprinted with permission from Holland & Hart.

Sample Fee Proposal for Real Estate Development reprinted with permission from Quarles & Brady, LLP.

Nothing contained in this book is to be considered as the rendering of legal advice for specific cases, and readers are responsible for obtaining such advice from their own legal counsel. This book and any forms and agreements herein are intended for educational and informational purposes only.

The products and services mentioned in this publication are under or may be under trademark or service mark protection. Product and service names and terms are used throughout only in an editorial fashion, to the benefit of the product manufacturer or service provider, with no intention of infringement. Use of a product or service name or term in this publication should not be regarded as affecting the validity of any trademark or service mark.

The Law Practice Management Section, American Bar Association, offers an educational program for lawyers in practice. Books and other materials are published in furtherance of that program. Authors and editors of publications may express their own legal interpretations and opinions, which are not necessarily those of either the American Bar Association or the Law Practice Management Section unless adopted pursuant to the bylaws of the Association. The opinions expressed do not reflect in any way a position of the Section or the American Bar Association.

Library of Congress Control Number 2003108784
ISBN-10: 1-60442-128-2
ISBN-13: 978-1-60442-128-6

11 10 09 08   5 4 3 2 1

Library of Congress Cataloging-in-Publication Data
Winning Alternatives to the Billable Hour, 3rd Edition. Mark A. Robertson and James A. Calloway: Library of Congress Cataloging-in-Publication Data is on file.

Discounts are available for books ordered in bulk. Special consideration is given to state bars, CLE programs, and other bar-related organizations. Inquire at Book Publishing, American Bar Association, 321 N. Clark Street, Chicago, Illinois 60654.

Contents

CHAPTER SIX
Developing the Case Plan or Transaction Plan   **71**

CHAPTER SEVEN
Implementing Value-Based Billing   **77**

About the Authors

Mark A. Robertson is a lawyer with the law firm of Robertson & Williams in Oklahoma City. His practice is focused on corporate and securities law and representing businesses and the families that own them. He received his B.A. degree from DePauw University and his J.D. from the University of Oklahoma College of Law. He also attended the University of Edinburgh, where he studied international law.

Mr. Robertson is a member of the Oklahoma and American Bar Associations. He is a past Chair of the ABA Law Practice Management Section and a Fellow and Trustee of the College of Law Practice Management. He is on the Editorial Board and has served as the articles editor and the columns editor for *Law Practice Management,* published by the ABA Law Practice Management Section. He has also served on the Publishing Board for the Law Practice Management Section. He is currently a delegate from the Law Practice Management Section to the ABA House of Delegates.

Mr. Robertson is a frequent lecturer on small and mid-sized law firm marketing and management issues and is a contributing author on law firm management topics to various national, state, and local bar association publications.

Jim Calloway is a lawyer who currently serves as the director of the Oklahoma Bar Association Management Assistance Program. He received his J.D. from the University of Oklahoma, where he was named to the Oklahoma Law Review.

Mr. Calloway is a member of the American Bar Association, where he has served as Chair of ABA TECHSHOW®. He is an active member of the ABA Law Practice Management Section, serves on its Council and is on its Practice Management Advisors Committee. He is also an active member of the ABA's General Practice, Solo and Small Firm Section, where he has served as Technology Chair for the Solo and Small Firm Division and served on the Web site committee for the National Association of Bar Executives. As a part of his duties with the OBA, he manages the OBA-NET, the official online service of the Oklahoma Bar. He has made numerous presentations on law office management, legal technology, ethics, and legal business operations. He also manages the annual OBA Solo and Small Firm Conference.

Before taking his present position with the OBA, he was in private practice for approximately sixteen years in south Oklahoma City and Norman. He is a former president of the Cleveland County Bar Association. He is a member of the Oklahoma City PC Users Group and, back in the pre-Internet era, ran a computer bulletin board for lawyers and those wishing to discuss legal issues called the Barrister's Club BBS.

Mr. Calloway has been a featured speaker at many prominent legal technology and legal management conferences. He has also spoken at bar association meetings in a number of states. His articles have been published in numerous legal publications.

Acknowledgments

Sir Isaac Newton stated about the process of the scientific discovery, "If I have seen further, it is by standing on the shoulders of giants."

That observation is well applied to the book you hold in your hands. Leaders and forward-thinkers of the ABA Law Practice Management Section recognized long before many others the illogical and contradictory nature of attorney billing based solely on an hourly basis. This book is another link in the chain of a series of works on this topic.

The creation of the Task Force on Alternative Billing Methods by the ABA Law Practice Management Section in 1987 ultimately resulted in four prior publications on this subject: *Beyond the Billable Hour: An Anthology of Alternative Billing Methods,* published in 1989; *Win-Win Billing Strategies: Alternatives That Satisfy Your Clients and You,* published in 1992; *Billing Innovations: New Win-Win Ways to End Hourly Billing,* published in 1996; and *Winning Alternatives to the Billable Hour: Strategies that Work* published in 2002. To all of the many individuals who contributed, we owe a great deal of thanks—none more than the late Richard C. Reed, chair of the task force, who contributed greatly to three of the publications as editor and author. Dick Reed built the foundation upon which everything written in this book rests.

Special thanks go to Debby Lee and Kirby Sadler for many hours of proofing and editorial assistance. Thanks also to Beverly Loder for her encouragement in doing this edition and for Tim Johnson for shepherding us through. Finally, Mark Robertson would like to gratefully acknowledge and thank his wife, Susan, and sons, Matthew and David, for their support and understanding, allowing him to work on this book even during what should have been "their" time. Jim Calloway would like to thank his wife, Terri, for proofreading as well as tolerance, and his son, Tanner, who thinks he contributed greatly to this book, since all the work was done at home and he heard far too many times, "No, Daddy is working on his book."

Introduction

> "A gunfighter doesn't charge by the bullet."
> —*Poster in well-known criminal defense lawyer's office*

This book will examine alternative billing methods for lawyers—whether practicing in a large firm, small firm or as a solo practitioner. How do we distinguish the lawyer's perception of value from the client's perception? How should we price services? How do we build an alternative billing method, and how does technology play into that? We will discuss tools to use in your practice to implement and evaluate alternative billing methods, and we will give you real case studies of lawyers and firms successfully using alternative billing to deliver value to both the client and the lawyer.

As most of you know, there are many legal services that lawyers provide that are not billed on an hourly basis at all. There are many cases handled on contingency fee. These often include plaintiff's personal injury claims, worker's compensation claims, and collection cases. There are many cases handled on percentage fees. Some examples of these can be probate cases, professional service contracts for athletes, authors, and entertainers, corporate mergers, and initial public offerings of stock. Many consumer matters are handled on a flat fee basis, like drafting of simple wills, uncontested bankruptcies, real estate closings, and the like.

So why is hourly billing considered the norm while all these other forms of determining lawyer fees are "alternative?"

Is it because lawyers have always done it that way? No, hourly billing is a relatively recent method of determining fees. One doesn't really think of Abraham Lincoln filling out time sheets and filing them next to his Blackstone's Commentaries, nor does one imagine in the pre-computer and pre-calculator days, the lawyer meticulously recording his time by the tenth of an hour to calculate the amount to bill for services.

Is it because hourly billing is popular among clients? That is certainly not true for individual consumers and is increasingly not true for business-people. Imagine that your local clothing store or appliance dealer set prices like lawyers often set their legal fees. "Well, the price for this suit really depends on a lot of factors: how much our supplier decides to charge for cloth, how long it takes me to measure and fit you for the suit, how much time it takes the tailor to make the suit, the shipping costs to get it here, and the time it takes to do the final alterations. But if you will agree to pay, then we will deliver you a suit and tell you the price when we are finished!"

Hourly fees became popular because such fees are easily determined by lawyers and easily reviewed by clients; they are clear, unambiguous and perceived by many to be objective and definite! Technology and accounting systems made it possible to track time and easily multiply the time by a rate to arrive at a fee.

One can imagine some insurance company or corporate executive examining bills for legal services and questioning why one matter cost twice as much as another matter when the matters were exactly the same. The response was that one took a lot more time, and the rejoinder was that then there should be time records to review. After all, the business paid its employees by the hour. The concept made sense. It is objective. It is unambiguous.

Once there are more than a few lawyers in a firm, the firm needs to have some measurement of productivity. So in one fell swoop, hourly billing met both the client's needs for an objective measurement of the cost of their legal services and the law firm's needs to manage and quantify lawyer production and value to the firm.

Frankly, hourly billing has worked very well for many years and will continue to be utilized in many situations. Business clients became acclimated to receiving these types of bills. Even in many consumer cases there was a certain fairness in the method. The divorce client who insisted on calling his lawyer every few days (or nights) was appropriately charged more than a less time-consuming client.

Advances in technology have clearly changed the status quo. From the first IBM typewriter with memory to the latest computer network, the modern tools of the trade of the law office allow us not only to track our time but to produce our documents more quickly and easily. The time involved for other tasks is reduced as well. The result of combining a reduction in the time for production of an individual document with an adherence to a hourly billing method is a drop in the fees charged for a particular task. This is by now no surprise to the lawyers reading this book.

The question that needs to be asked is whether the value of legal services has decreased just because the methods of production have improved. Is a Last Will and Testament that bore a value of $350 in the legal marketplace now reduced in value because the lawyer has invested effort, energy and expense in creating a document-drafting system that substantially reduces the preparation time for this important document? We believe that the value of the Last Will to the consumer is based on the quality and appropriateness of the document based on the lawyer's analysis of this client's circumstances, not on the mechanics of its creation.

In fact, the actual time personally contributed to a task by the lawyer can be almost meaningless in regard to the value of the product. A very narrow and specialized medical malpractice case might require dozens of hours of research, consultation with experts and careful drafting just to prepare interrogatories. When the lawyer has prepared and tried four or five of these types of cases, preparation of interrogatories based on the prior work product might take less than an hour or two for some customization based on the specific facts of any new case. Would anyone doubt that, based on the experience of the lawyer, the interrogatories in the newest case were superior to those propounded in the first case, even though they took less time to draft?

Experience improves the lawyer's work product and abilities. As experience allowed an individual to perform tasks more efficiently and quickly, the traditional response was to raise the person's hourly billing rate. Therefore associates charge one rate, while junior and senior partners charge another. However, as many lawyers have come to realize, upward hourly rate adjustments are not always possible. Experience may not always be rewarded with higher rates. If the medical malpractice lawyer mentioned above charged $2,200 for the first interrogatories prepared (10 hours at $220 per hour), can he raise his hourly rate to $1,100 per hour for the two hours it took him to do the interrogatories in the fifth case? Is it ethical for him to "pad" his time to reflect 10 hours work when he only had two?

Technology allows for the easy reuse of the lawyer's prior work product, whether through forms or document assembly systems. Technology also allows one to perform tasks more quickly and efficiently. Should technology be used to just reduce the fees charged to clients based upon the time it takes to now perform a task, or should the benefit of these efficiencies be shared between the lawyer and client?

If the result of the implementation of technology only means less lawyer time invested, which equals less compensation, then a logical conclusion would be for lawyers to avoid improving their practices through the use of technology. We all know that proper implementation of technology also improves our work product, eliminating typographical errors and freeing up trained staff from mind-numbing repetitive work to concentrate on more important tasks. But should this be done if it penalizes the lawyer whose fees are determined only by the hours spent?

Our clients expect their lawyers to use the best and latest practice methods. They have a right to expect it. Systems developed to save time and resources and proper uses of technology save money for law firms and clients alike. Compare the cost and efficiency of using a fax machine for sending a document across the country or around the globe as opposed to using the mail or a courier service. Now compare the cost savings of sending an e-mail attachment of the document as opposed to a long-distance fax.

So, we are going to use technology to deliver the best possible product to our clients, but at what cost to our livelihood? The paradox is that the focus of most technology in the law practice is to decrease the time it takes to accomplish a task. The more productive you become using technology, the less income you make if you bill only by the hour! The value to the client has not changed (or if it has, it has gone up, since the service is more immediate), so why should the charges for such legal services be less?

It seems that the benefits of technology and systems designed to help us work more efficiently should accrue both to the client and the lawyer—especially when the lawyer has to invest money, effort and time into harnessing technology and establishing systems.

There are many forces that inhibit the implementation of alternative billing practices from both the client's and lawyer's points of view. In fact, the adoption of many of these practices has been much slower than predicted by many who were examining these concepts nearly two decades ago. But there can be no doubt that these changes are coming. The practice of outsourcing basic research or contract drafting offshore to foreign law firms in India and elsewhere is driving law firms to review how they charge for such work. General counsels of corporations are starting to look at alternative ways to manage costs. Insurance companies in particular have been initiating new fee-setting arrangements with their counsel that would have been improbable a decade ago. It is also noteworthy that many consider insurance defense practice less lucrative than some years ago. How many of those lawyers would have been better prepared to deal with proposals of new fee arrangements with an understanding of the concepts contained in this book?

Reading this book may not change your law practice or your billing practices overnight. But challenges to the "hourly only" billing practices will continue. Maybe the challenge will occur in the form of your best client proposing a restructuring of the fee arrangement. Do you now have the tools in hand to properly analyze all of the implications of such a proposal? Maybe the challenge will occur when a new lawyer fresh out of law school opens a practice down the street from you, charging an extremely low price for certain routine legal work that you now perform. You may believe it is impossible to competently handle such matters at such a rate, while the new lawyer views these services as only filling in a few blanks in a form and printing the document. Maybe the challenge will occur when a judge or agency limits the fees that can be charged for a certain service.

No one should have a better understanding of how much it costs to produce services than the lawyer who depends on billing for those services to make his or her livelihood. It is imperative that the lawyer be prepared to cope with future challenges, whether from those outside the law firm or from systemic changes in the manner that legal services are provided. The purpose of this book is to inform, stimulate thinking and provide some tools for the lawyer to deal with the inevitable challenges and future business decisions that will need to be made in this area.

Hourly billing is not an inherently evil practice. In fact, certain types of tasks that are time intensive and outside of the law firm's control may still best be billed on a hourly basis. But one can also conclude that the economic pressures and challenges will continue to build. Is a complaint filed in court devalued because the firm's expertise in the area, combined with its technology, allows assembly of the complaint in a much shortened time frame? Is the only path for a law firm to increase profitability to either raise the billing rates or hire more associates?

Whether you call it alternative billing, value billing, fixed-fee billing, or task-based billing, the time has come to examine how to fairly charge for legal services so that the outcome can be "win-win" for everyone.

The Search for the Meaning of Value

1

Value is an elusive quality, but discussing billing methods is impossible without considering the "value" received and perceived by the client. That is why this book and the two prior editions start with the meaning of value in billing for our services. This book is intended to be practical. But implementation of alternative billing will depend on a number of individual factors and considerations. In making these decisions in your law practice, understanding the meaning of value is required.

From the standpoint of the client, the value of legal services is the client's perception that there has been a benefit. Value may be positive in the sense of acquiring a desired result, but value may also be a negative, such as the avoidance of a detriment or risk, as in the successful defense of a civil or criminal case. When the price of the services received reflects the client's perception of value, the client will be satisfied.

Lawyers and Clients: Perception Is Reality

One of the key points in discussing value is to understand that there are frequent differences in perception between the lawyer's point of view and the client's point of view. Lawyers are trained to make calculations on probable outcomes and risks. The lawyers may not consciously calculate the odds in a mathematical fashion in all client matters and may resist reducing a complex situation to a stated probability or percentage. But in many situations the client and lawyer can only communicate in terms of possibilities when trying to make appropriate decisions.

Lawyers frequently deal with dozens of these future judgments every day and in every matter. Will the jury believe a certain witness? Will the judge view the case as more analogous to precedent A or precedent B? Will the taxing authorities oppose or accept a certain proposed tax treatment? What dollar amount of damages might a jury award for a certain injury in a certain region of the country? What sentence will the judge impose for a certain offense? What type of zoning change both serves the client's proposed use and is most likely to be approved by the municipal authorities? Will a certain document be deemed admissible into evidence or excluded?

If a lawyer is pinned down and forced to give some sort of odds, the client may view them very differently from the lawyer. Telling a client there is a 60 percent chance of success may give him the idea that "our attorney said we will probably win." The lawyer, on the other hand, is thinking that it is a toss-up, with a slight advantage to the client's benefit. Stating that the odds are 90 to 10 in a client's favor leaves the client with the idea that victory is assured, while the lawyer still understands that if ten of these cases with these exact facts are tried, one will be lost.

Therefore the lawyer may counsel that paying $100,000 to settle a one-in-ten chance of losing a $1,000,000 is a rational decision, especially when one considers the attorney fees that will be incurred on the way to that court date. The client may be aghast at the prospect of paying $100,000 to settle a sure winner, especially when the attorney's fees that have already been incurred to date are considered.

The possibility of a disconnect between the lawyer's perception and the client's perception is a critical concern in all aspects of the attorney-client relationship, and that includes setting fees and billing.

Client Perceptions of Value

Clients perceive value in a variety of ways. When spending money adds to the value of what a person has, the dollar outlay is an investment, not an expense. A developer client invests in raw land, hoping to have it rezoned as a residential subdivision. The developer pays for planning and engineering services to lay out the tract, for a lawyer whose expertise results in appropriate rezoning, and for streets and utilities to be installed. Each of these investments adds value to the developer's land. They are clear and, in a sense, tangible.

Individuals would prefer to achieve a result or to conserve existing assets. Businesses would prefer to invest capital in assets upon which there will be a return. Thus, both individuals and businesses would prefer not to pay legal expenses unless there is a benefit. For example, an individual client may wish to have an estate plan that will provide for family needs with minimum tax impacts, or a business client may want to collect a past-due account. Where the client's objectives are reached, value has been achieved.

But perceptions are affected by many factors. A client's prejudices, experiences, cultural background, social and economic status, religious background, or education all may impact the client's perception of a legal matter. A client sued for divorce who does not want the divorce will often never appreciate fully the valuable advice and counsel of the lawyer. The same is true for a businessperson who is sued over a course of conduct that he or she deemed proper.

What Is Value?

Lawyers sometimes tend to take for granted the many ways that they bring value to their clients and the transactions in which they are involved. After a transaction becomes somewhat routine, a lawyer may underestimate the experience, and therefore the value, he or she brings to bear on a legal need.

The following examples illustrating how clients perceive value, while not exhaustive, should stimulate the lawyer's thinking and also provide a reference source for the future should a lawyer be challenged as to his or her value:

- ◆ Avoiding exposure to risk (or possible ruin), such as losing all assets or going to jail, is value. Thus, lawyers can provide value in the form of enabling a successful corporate reorganization or a not-guilty verdict in a criminal case.
- ◆ Sometimes a brilliant idea or insight can produce great value, even though it results from a small amount of time. A simple solution to a complex and seemingly unsolvable problem occasionally results from a restructuring of the problem posed, from a burst of brilliance, or from the deep experience of the counseling lawyer.
- ◆ The ongoing process of supporting a client's needs can represent value. The lawyer's routine handling of a client's ongoing needs in a complex society gives the client peace of mind and frees him or her to pursue other ends, whether personal or financial. Representation by a strong, competent, loyal, well-established, and highly regarded lawyer can bring stability and credibility to the client's life.

◆ Wisdom is an elusive concept. But clearly a maturity of judgment, a steady hand, and a restraint on impulsive actions can translate to immense value. The lawyer's ability to persuade against unsound courses of action or in favor of preventive action may be of great benefit to the client.

◆ The lawyer's acceptance of responsibility can produce value. In high-risk transactions, having a competent lawyer act with knowledge of the risks involved and with a willingness to put his or her reputation on the line may in itself be value.

◆ The ability to communicate can be a source of value when used to help clients understand what is occurring or what is planned. To many clients, legal matters are a mystery. Consequently, the lawyer's ability to speak in terms that clients can understand helps dispel the mystery.

◆ Timely performance is value. Clients, too, have time schedules and appreciate services that are timely. Providing prompt service demonstrates that the lawyer gives priority to the client.

◆ High-level specialized expertise and skill create value. Some matters require unique skills and experience. In those situations, clients will seek out lawyers who provide highly valued specialized services.

◆ Exclusivity or unavailability to others can be value. The traditional retainer to ensure availability shows that clients recognize the importance of having a lawyer or law firm available in case they need legal services. The lawyer can serve as the client's anchor when the need for legal services arises, even if those needs only arise from time to time. Long-standing relationships are usually the foundation for successful law practice.

◆ A timely follow-up to see that there are no loose ends can be a most important source of value. Most clients want the transaction completed and the matter terminated, and they become restive when most but not all of the necessary steps are taken.

◆ A straightforward approach can be a very appreciated value. Lawyers provide value when they do only what is needed. This may include advising a client that nothing need be done, telling the client how to proceed without the involvement or expense of the lawyer, or finding a simple solution. Simple solutions are, by their very nature, often under-rated and under-valued. But providing a reasonably acceptable solution, even though deluxe alternatives might be available, is a true mark of professionalism and value when the client only needs a reasonably acceptable product.

◆ Guaranteeing satisfaction is certainly value. Clients stick with a lawyer when they know that he or she will "make it right" in terms of what is done or what is charged.

Dependability, integrity, evenness of performance, reliability of product, personal and professional stability, and many other factors all constitute value. A lawyer should never underestimate his or her value, whether as a recent entry into the legal marketplace or as a seasoned veteran.

Conclusion

All of the benefits named in this chapter, when viewed from the standpoint of the client's perceptions, are elements of value that create the basis for determining what the client will be willing to pay. As we shall see, two other factors affect value and the client's perception of value. The first is supply and demand. The second is communication, the ability of lawyer and client to understand each other throughout the whole of their relationship. The lawyer must understand the client's problems and needs and take appropriate actions, but in today's marketplace, it is not enough to merely provide value. It is incumbent upon the successful lawyer to deliver value, to communicate to the client the value that has been delivered, and to endeavor to insure that the client's perception of the value received is in line with the perception of the lawyer.

Ethical Rules and Practices

2

*Special rules and restrictions relate to lawyers and the fees
they may charge. Even the most innovative billing method
must comply with those ethical rules and practices. Each
lawyer must make certain that the fees charged and the
methods of billing comply with the applicable requirements in the states where they practice.*

The Basic Rule

Although each jurisdiction's ethical rules and court decisions
vary, the American Bar Association's Model Rules of Professional
Conduct as amended in 2002 set forth the basic ground rules governing all fees. Rule 1.5, dealing with lawyers' fees, states, "A
lawyer shall not make an agreement for, charge, or collect an unreasonable fee. . . ." The rule goes on to set forth eight factors to
consider in determining the reasonableness of a fee:

1. The time and labor required, novelty and difficulty of the
   questions involved, and the skill requisite to perform the
   legal services properly.
2. The likelihood, if apparent to the client, that the acceptance of the assignment will preclude other employment
   by the lawyer.
3. The fee customarily charged in the locality for similar
   legal services.
4. The amount involved and results obtained.

5. The time limitation imposed by the client or by the circumstances.
6. The nature and length of the professional relationship with the client.
7. The experience, reputation, and ability of the lawyer or lawyers performing the services.
8. Whether the fee is fixed or contingent.

Rule 1.5 recommends that the fee agreement be in writing unless the lawyer regularly represents the client. If the fee is contingent, then the agreement *must* be in writing, signed by the client, and set forth the method by which the fee is determined, including the percentage accruing to the lawyer if the matter is settled, tried, or appealed; litigation expenses to be deducted; and whether the deduction is made before or after the contingent fee is calculated. Also, upon conclusion of the matter, the lawyer charging a contingent fee must provide a written statement of the outcome. If there is a recovery, the lawyer must also provide an accounting establishing the basis for the remittance to the client.

The rule further provides that contingent fee agreements are not permitted in criminal matters or in domestic relations matters involving the securing of a dissolution, support, or property settlements in lieu of support. The comments to Rule 1.5 provides that contingent fees, like any other fees, are subject to a reasonableness standard.

Finally, the rule addresses the question of fee splitting between lawyers. Lawyers who are not members of the same firm may not split fees unless all three of the following criteria are met:

1. The division is in proportion to the services performed or each lawyer assumes joint responsibility for the representation;
2. The client agrees to the arrangement, including the share each lawyer will receive, and the agreement is confirmed in writing; and
3. The total fee is reasonable.

The commentary to Rule 1.5 states that a lawyer may require an advance payment of a fee, subject to remitting any unearned fee balance to the client. Whether the lawyer should place such fees into a trust account to be withdrawn as earned is governed by Rule 1.15 and will be discussed later.

Rule 1.5 goes on to provide that the lawyer may accept property, including an ownership interest in an enterprise. However, the lawyer may not accept an interest in the subject matter of the litigation or have a proprietary interest in the cause of action except to the extent a lien is granted by law securing the lawyer's fees or as permitted in contingency fee matters. A lawyer entering into a business transaction with a client should review Rule 1.8(a), which governs such conduct.

Because fees are an area of great concern to lawyers, courts, legislators, clients, and the public, each jurisdiction develops its own particular version of acceptable conduct and standards with respect to fees. To confuse matters more, ethics opinions spelling out what is acceptable or required vary from jurisdiction to jurisdiction. Even jurisdictions that have adopted the American Bar Association (ABA) rules often modify Rule 1.5, or the rule is later modified by court decision or the legislature may enact legislation that differs from the rule.

Some jurisdictions require mandatory fee arbitration. Others make it available, and still other jurisdictions are silent on the subject or apply it only to certain types of cases, matters, or substantive areas of law.

Some jurisdictions have specific requirements with respect to types of fee agreements such as contingency fees. Some require that certain conditions or provisions be met with respect to those fees. Some limit the requirements to specific types of cases or prohibit certain types of fee agreements in particular kinds of cases, or some set forth maximum fees or caps that the lawyer may not exceed.

Familiarity with the local ethical rules may bring comfort to the law firm. But when law firms expand across state lines, variations on acceptable fee agreements from jurisdiction to jurisdiction compromise their ability to fashion standard fee agreements that can be used throughout the various jurisdictions.

The Golden Rule

It is important to consider that even if a fee agreement is signed by a sophisticated client and sets a fee that is within the "going rate," it may not be acceptable. The underlying principle is that the fees charged must be *reasonable*. Although the eight factors listed above are a guide in determining reasonableness, other factors may be considered by a court reviewing the fee. The bottom line is that the overall fee charged must be reasonable when measured against the benefits received by the client, even if this standard appears to involve a certain amount of hindsight and regardless of whether the fee is value based or hourly.

To illustrate, imagine that you have a written contract with a knowledgeable client at a fixed reasonable hourly rate resulting in a fee of $50,000 over a dispute involving an issue worth only $25,000. You will have difficulty in sustaining the fee in the face of client objection. If your fee is "the going rate" in your community, but nevertheless unreasonable, you will have difficulty obtaining approval of the fee by the court over a client's objection. In spite of contract terms, time expended, client sophistication, or any of the other factors you may look to in justifying or rationalizing the fee, it all comes down to one question: Is the fee reasonable?

Therefore it is important to understand that a lawyer does not have complete freedom to enter into a contract with a client for any amount of fees. A client who is satisfied with the representation and outcome may gladly pay the fee no matter what the amount. But if there is a situation where the client disputes the fee or a court must approve it, there is the potential for second guessing. Bluntly put, these provisions of Rule 1.5 strip the lawyer of unfettered freedom to set fees himself and give the court the authority to set them at a level that the court thinks is appropriate. So if a judge believes that the attorney is "gouging" the client, there will be ample rationalization in the factors of the rule to support a fee reduction. On the other hand, most fees can be supported by the factors contained therein if the court is inclined to do so.

Gray Areas

Although each jurisdiction has its own rules, court opinions, and procedures as well as possible legislative enactments governing fee agreements between lawyers and their clients, there are some controversial areas where ethicists disagree. These are currently in a state of flux.

Prepaid Fees in Lawyer's Trust Account

One such problem area is the question of whether lawyers who receive fees from clients in advance for work to be done in the future should put those prepaid fees into a trust account. For example, a client pays you a fixed fee to form a corporation or to defend a criminal charge. Should you put the funds you receive into a trust account to be withdrawn as the work is completed? What if the fee received is a payment on account of fees and the agreement is that you will bill against the deposited fee as the work is done—should you deposit that fee into a trust account? What if the initial fee you receive is not refundable or only partially refundable and you are to bill against the fees on deposit—should you deposit the entire fee into a trust account or only the portion above the amount that is not refundable, or should you put the entire amount of the fee into a trust account and take money out as you earn the fees?

Some jurisdictions have addressed one or more of these questions. See, for example, the State Bar of California Standing Committee on Professional Responsibility and Conduct Formal Opinion No. 1990-121 and San Francisco Bar Association Ethics Opinion No. 1980-1. Also, articles have been written on this subject, including Shank, "Are Advance Fee Payments Clients' Funds?" 55 *Cal. S.B.J.* 370 (1980); Dimitriou, "Should Prepaid Fees Be Put in a Trust Account?" *California Lawyer*, Vol. 6, No. 2, p. 20 (1983); Brickman and Cunningham, "Non-refundable Retainers: Impermissible under Fiduciary Statutory and Contract Law," 57 *Fordham Law Review* 149 (1988); and Brickman, "The Advance Fee Payment Dilemma: Should Payments Be Deposited to the Client Trust Account or to the General Office Account?" 10 *Cardozo Law Review* 647 (1989). See also the comprehensive treatise on trust accounting published by the American Bar Association, Law Practice Management Section, entitled *The ABA Guide to Lawyer Trust Accounts* by Jay G Foonberg (1996).

These writers do not speak with a single voice. How these questions would be answered in a particular jurisdiction is beyond the scope of this chapter.

Fee Agreements in Writing

Opinions also differ on the need for a fee agreement to be in writing. ABA Rule 1.5 requires that a fee agreement be in writing only in contingent fee matters, and the effort by the ABA's Ethics 2000 Commission to require all fee arrangements over $500 to be in writing failed to pass in the House of Delegates when it was presented in February 2002. However, the commentary to the rule suggests that, in an effort to reduce the possibility of client misunderstanding, the fee agreement be reduced to writing when the lawyer has not regularly represented the client (the rule itself provides that in such circumstances, the fee arrangement shall be "communicated to the client").

Like the ABA rule, jurisdictions differ as to whether a written fee agreement need be used only in contingent fee matters. Some jurisdictions require that all fee agreements be in writing, and some only if the fee is expected to be over a certain dollar minimum. Some require a written agreement only in certain types of contingent fee matters, and some have no special requirements relating to contingent fees. Again, you must review local rules, court opinions, ethics opinions, and laws.

Even though we acknowledge differing opinions among scholars concerning the question of which fee agreements are required to be in writing, we are of the opinion that sound business practices will dictate that fee agreements should be in writing in almost every situation. Written fee agreements allow the attorney the opportunity to formalize the representations of the attorney and financial arrangements. Experienced lawyers note that many a potential fee dispute has been silenced by reference to the written (and signed) fee agreement.

Mandatory Arbitration

Could your fee agreement include a provision that requires mandatory arbitration of any fee or malpractice dispute? At least one ethics opinion and one appellate court opinion have indicated that such a provision, as related to malpractice, may not be permissible. However, both suggest that if the arbitration provision is clearly worded and would put the client on notice concerning the detriments of the provision (e.g., loss of the right to a jury trial and the right to select a judicial forum), such a provision would be permitted. Various jurisdictions have passed laws establishing procedures for arbitration concerning attorneys' fees and imposing limits on contractual provisions. This is an area in which there is currently very little guidance but much interest.

Business Interests Received in Payment

Lawyers also find themselves in difficulty with clients over fees in instances where as payment, a lawyer accepts property such as an ownership interest in an enterprise or other property where reasonable people can differ as to the value. Accepting "a piece of the deal" of a new business may seem very logical to both the attorney and the entrepreneur as a way to accomplish legal goals while preserving often limited cash. Care should be taken to review Rule 1.8(a), which provides that the lawyer should take certain steps to protect the client when entering into a business transaction with that client.

But this can create a problem if the client later objects and attempts to apply an after-the-fact analysis. The client may never object to the lawyer's fractional interest in a business enterprise that becomes worthless. But if an enterprise succeeds spectacularly, then the lawyer risks having to defend a claim by the client that the resulting fee is unreasonable. There is disagreement among commentators on whether this is a permissible fee arrangement.

Furthermore, a practical effect of accepting an interest in a business enterprise or other asset in lieu of fees is that the lawyer and client become "business partners," thus creating the potential for a future conflict of interest between the lawyer and the client. Model Rule 1.7 is concerned with in part, conflicts between a lawyer's own interests and the client's interest. A lawyer shall not represent a client if the representation of that client may be materially limited by the lawyer's own interests in a transaction unless (1) the lawyer reasonably believes that the lawyer will be able to provide competent and diligent representation to each affected client; (2) the representation is not prohibited by law; and (3) each affected client gives informed consent, confirmed in writing. Model Rule 1.8 is concerned with in part the ground rules that must be followed by a lawyer who accepts fees from a client in the form of property or property interests belonging to a client or who takes a security interest in property for payment of fees. Model Rule 1.8(a) provides that a lawyer shall not enter into a business transaction with a client or knowingly acquire an ownership, possessory, security or other pecuniary interest adverse to a client unless: (1) the transaction and terms on which the lawyer acquires the interest are fair and reasonable to the client and are fully disclosed and transmitted in writing in a manner that can be reasonably understood by the client; (2) the client is advised in writing of the desirability of seeking and is given a reasonable opportunity to seek the advice of independent legal counsel on the transaction; and (3) the client gives informed consent, in a writing signed by the client, to the essential terms of the transaction and the lawyer's role in the transaction, including whether the lawyer is representing the client in the transaction. The Ethics 2000 Commission added a significant amount of commentary to this Model Rule addressing issues of business transactions between client and lawyer, which comments were adopted by the House of Delegates in February, 2002.

Does a fee arrangement dependent upon a transaction closing violate Model Rule 2.1 requiring the lawyer to exercise independent professional judgment? One court found that the lawyer aided and abetted an SEC Rule 10b-5 violation by failing to act when the lawyer (who was also a shareholder, officer, and director of the business) stood to profit "handsomely" from the transaction. *SEC v. National Student Marketing Corp.* 457 F. Supp. 682 (D.D.C. 1978).

Each jurisdiction has created its own version of what is acceptable conduct for the lawyer in all these circumstances. While the Model Rules will focus you on the issues that need to be addressed, you must refer to the rules and opinions of your own jurisdiction for guidance on what is appropriate or safe conduct in these circumstances.

Conflicts

Although it was only touched upon earlier, it is important not only to be concerned with the underlying fairness of the fee but also to consider the issue of conflict of interest. This is important not only with respect to the amount of the fee, but also in every instance in which the fee is being paid by someone or some entity other than your client, e.g., friend, insurance company, or employer. See Model Rules 1.8(f) and 5.4(c). The conflict issue is also present and needs to be considered every time you have more than one client in the same matter.

Fee Sharing

Beyond the conflict issue are other important questions. These include the ethics of fee sharing among lawyers who are not members of the same firm (see the discussion above concerning Rule 1.5(e)). Even more thorny is the issue of fee splitting with nonlawyers. See Model Rule 5.4(a). Such fees may take the form of staff incentive bonuses, finder's fees, rental agreements based upon a percentage of gross fees, and other direct or indirect payments to a nonlawyer of a portion of the fees that the lawyer has earned or collected.

It behooves a lawyer to run each fee agreement through an ethics check, just as lawyers run each new client through a conflicts check. This is particularly true whenever the agreement concerns an unfamiliar or unusual area of practice, more than one client, or legal services in more than one jurisdiction.

Pricing Legal Services

3

*Too many lawyers may look at alternative billing methods
as a means of either making more money or doing less
work in the billing process. In fact, appropriate use of these
methods may ultimately result in one or both of those goals
and will focus everyone on value provided to the client. It
should be understood that there will be many hours invested in the transition from hourly to alternative billing
methods and fine-tuning alternative billing methods in the
future. This should be considered positive investment in
the future of the practice.*

*Whatever billing method you use, it is critical to know
the cost of producing legal services. Many factors, both theoretical and practical, go into the pricing of legal services.
Lawyers need to understand these factors to succeed in the
current legal environment.*

Historical Influences on Pricing Legal Services

How do our clients value our services? How should we price
those services both to reflect value to the client and to be able to
be profitable? No longer was the old English custom of slipping
money into the barrister's robe an acceptable method of compensating the barrister—the client and only the client determining the price to pay for the services. The practice of law is both
a profession and a business. In attempting to be more busi-

15

nesslike, lawyers over the last 30 years have used hours spent on matters as a measure of the value of those services

Pricing Before and After Bates

To understand why the concept of pricing is sometimes difficult for lawyers to understand, it is helpful to briefly review the nature of the legal profession before the landmark United States Supreme Court decision in *Bates & O'Steen v. State Bar of Arizona,* 433 U.S. 350 (1977), which enabled lawyers to market legal services.

For many years, lawyers would analyze the file (often at the end of the representation) and establish a fee based on the lawyer's determination of the value of the representation to the client. Establishing the fee was often as much art as science and was a skill a lawyer needed in order to survive. Gradually, minimum fee schedules were established by bar associations or common practice in the area. Then, roughly 45 years ago, experts using surveys of the legal profession found that lawyers who recorded their time earned more than those who didn't. Lawyers knew how much it cost to provide the services based on the time spent and could therefore set the fees appropriately. In the same general time period, because of possible antitrust violations, lawyers stopped using the traditional minimum-fee schedules. *Goldfarb v. Virginia State Bar*, 421 U.S. 773 (1975).

With the abolition of minimum-fee schedules and the experts and consultants telling lawyers that timekeeping was good, hourly billing rapidly evolved as a billing method of choice—particularly as law firms started to grow and it was an easy measure of the "value" of associates and increasing leverage for partners. Lawyers had been advised to keep time records in order to know the *cost* of providing services. No one said that billing solely on time was always appropriate, but the profession moved in the direction of multiplying time by an hourly rate to set fees. The time-rate method became predominant. The time spent on a matter moved from a measure of a lawyer's *cost* to a measure of a lawyer's *value*—hence hourly based bills. With the development of computerized record keeping and computerized billing, time had became the dominant basis for charging, and the transformation from value-based billing to time-based billing was complete. This was the case even though most computerized systems provided an opportunity for the billing lawyer to exercise judgment based on the value of the services to the client by writing up or writing down the initially calculated fee.

Detailed time records appealed to lawyers, clients, and the courts because they appeared to provide a tangible, objective means for setting fees. Contemporaneous time recording enabled the lawyer to produce a detailed transcript of what services had been provided. If effort was the major objective, time records could demonstrate with detailed descriptions all of the efforts that had been undertaken. The courts had some tangible evidence upon which to base a fee award. The semiautomatic business process of billing according to hours spent multiplied by hourly rate reduced the need of lawyers and judges to exercise discretion.

Constraints on the Marketplace

In classic economic terms, when supply exceeds demand, price declines. There are, however, some constraints on the free operation of the marketplace for the legal profession, both positive and negative. Some would argue that prices for legal services are inflated by the monopolistic effects of requiring licensure of lawyers as professionals for delivery of certain services. Several provisions of our ethical rules (discussed in Chapter Two) impose artificial constraints on the operation of the market. For example, no contingent fees are permitted in criminal and matrimonial matters, and every fee, irrespective of the billing method, must be "reasonable."

The operation of the marketplace is also affected by the client's perception of value. For that perception to be accurate, the client should be educated and informed as to what he or she needs to purchase and is purchasing. Some clients are unsophisticated and uneducated as to the legal process, so they need the protection of the ethical constraints. However, some clients are highly sophisticated purchasers of legal services and, in a buyer's market, can exert extreme pressure on price because of the leveraging that results from having high volumes of work to assign to outside counsel. Across the range of unsophisticated to sophisticated purchasers of legal service, perceptions of value may differ.

Historically, most lawyers and law firms determined price on a subjective or rule-of-thumb basis, taking into account some or all of the following factors: inflation, costs, and the desired level of profit or income. With a declining amount of law work available, an increased number of lawyers, combined with increased and more direct competition through marketing, clients saw other providers as alternatives to their traditional legal counsel, thereby forcing lawyers to be less casual about billing methods. To remain competitive for the future, more careful internal study is warranted for fee pricing.

The Modern Focus on Value

Tying lawyers' fees to hourly billing tends to force lawyers to perceive all matters as being of equal importance. But all matters are not of equal importance and value. Lawyers perceive value as a function of the hourly rate and effort; clients do not. If the lawyer enables a client to acquire a $200 million company for $10 million less than the client expected, the lawyer's fee of $30,000 easily seems appropriate. On the other hand, if the client's perception is that the lawyer was merely to draft the paperwork for a deal that had already been negotiated between the companies, this fee may seem extreme. The difference is the perception of value. With the hourly billing approach, the lawyer need not get involved in understanding the client's value system and business, because hourly billing "should be" an accepted practice. How much ribbing will this lawyer get from some of the hourly martyrs in the firm who ask, "Couldn't you have been less efficient, used more associates and hours, and developed a higher fee?" A classic situation comes to mind, in which the partner asked why the firm needed to invest in a litigation system when it would just make the lawyers more efficient, reducing the fees and therefore the firm's profit. Lawyers who base price on hourly billing rates will not be able to meet the following challenge: Reduce the client's legal fees *and* maintain quality *and* increase firm profitability.

In today's legal marketplace, the trend should be away from cost-based billing represented by hourly billing and toward billing methods that recognize that the client's perception of value should be a primary consideration. Client demand increasingly drivies pricing strategy and affects internal law firm responses regarding the manner in which services are provided.

In the business world, pricing is a profit-planning exercise in which management searches for alternative pricing policies and evaluates the profit consequences of various alternatives before reaching a pricing decision. Increasingly, attorneys must understand the relationship between the value of services in the market, the internal costs of production, the fees set, and the effect of alternative billing methods on profitability.

Given the more client-driven market, lawyers must understand and respond to a client's desires for predictability and value in order to succeed in the marketplace. One should know enough about one's practice and obtain accurate information from the client to be able to answer the following questions:

- Should I take this case for the fee available?
- How much money will I make/lose if I take this case?
- Are the fees established by my competition too high or too low for my particular practice?
- Can I be more effective in choosing the tasks that would be performed and delegating work to less expensive lawyers and staff?
- Can I be more efficient, provide the same quality of service, and still make some money?
- Should I stop handling this type of case altogether?
- If I decide to take this case as a loss leader, just how much is my loss likely to be and what must I do to leverage the credibility gained into higher-profit future cases?
- Is my overhead unreasonably high, or is it low enough that I can compete and provide quality services in this type of work while still making some profit?
- What kind of cases, clients, or work produces the most/least net profit?

- Is the nature of my practice changing from year to year? If so, is it changing toward greater net profit or lesser net profit?
- Is one type of fee arrangement more profitable than another?

These questions are natural and appropriate from the point of view of your self-interest. However, you should answer them with an overriding concern for the value of your services to the client. How are you to know the client's perception of value? That is the fundamental threshold of each new case or matter—to understand each client's objectives. If you don't know client objectives, you will find it impossible to be confident that your services will meet those objectives and hence conform to the client's perception of value. You may also find you have trouble getting paid.

Ideally, your talents and skills should match exactly the client's needs or requirements. As a practical matter, this is difficult to achieve in many situations because lawyers are not all alike and the needs of clients vary.

Even a single client's needs or wants may vary from matter to matter. At times a form or routine service requiring only minimal skills may suffice. If so, the services may be performed by a nonlawyer supervised by a lawyer. At other times the client may need highly skilled services that can be provided only by a lawyer with high-level expertise.

As an analogy, consider the purchase of clothing. Some buyers want quality; others are more concerned with price. Some are interested in prestige or the label. Some buyers are concerned about fad and fashion, while others don't care. Likewise, when selecting a restaurant, some customers want fine dining, where atmosphere and location may be very important. Other customers may prefer good food served in a simple eatery. Sometimes a customer may want a five-course meal, at other times a bowl of soup, a cup of coffee, or a hamburger.

Regardless of how price is determined, it has upper and lower limits. The upper limit is usually apparent when the price is so high that hardly anyone wants to or can afford to purchase the good or service. Few purchases also result when a price is so low that it raises concerns about quality and value. If the price is higher than the client's perception of value, the client will seek other solutions by altering the process, going outside the system, or seeking other lawyers to serve his or her needs.

The Value Curve

The price of a service or the billing rate for the service must reflect the value perceived by the client. The law firm can no longer set its billing rates and price its work in a vacuum; it must have an intimate working knowledge of the client's business and value system.

Herbert Maslow, an eminent industrial psychologist, once said, "If the only tool you have is a hammer, everything begins to look like a nail." In the legal profession, we need a tool for pricing services. William C. Cobb of Cobb Consulting of Houston, Texas has developed and popularized the "value curve" as such a tool. It supplements the hourly rate or cost-based billing and can identify areas where the client's perception of value is not tied to the hours a lawyer spends on the matter.

The value curve (and competitive position profile), which is illustrated in Figure 3-1, shows the relative value of services versus the volume of the work available to a law firm. The greater the volume of available work (horizontal axis), the more lawyers that can capably perform the work. The more lawyers there are to perform the work, the more price-sensitive is the service. In other words, when customers (clients) can shop around, they will look for a low price. The curve may be compared to a product life cycle. The longer a profitable product is around in the market, the more producers will enter the market to produce price competition. For example, look what has happened to the personal computer. Prices started in the range of $3,000 to $4,000 and have come down, with the increased number of producers in the market, to as low as $400 to $600. Legal services will not escape the laws of economics.

The vertical axis of Figure 3-1 shows the relative value of the service. The greater the perceived value to the client, the higher the position on the line.

Figure 3-1   Value Curve (Competitive Position Profile)

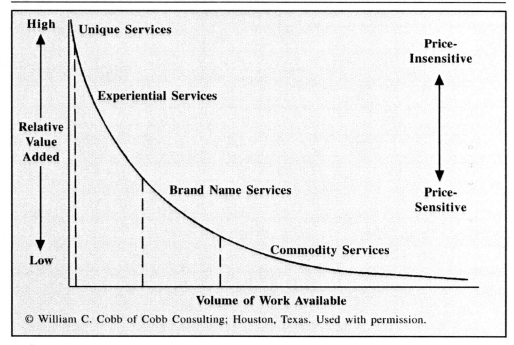

© William C. Cobb of Cobb Consulting; Houston, Texas. Used with permission.

Value may be added by the client's perception of the lawyer's worth, availability, timeliness, prestige, and other factors discussed in Chapter One. As the value moves from high to low, the client becomes more sensitive to price.

Interpreting the Curve

For clarity, the value curve is segmented into four classifications of work:

1. *Unique.* This is a nuclear event to the client. Less than 4 percent of the work in a market is unique work.
2. *Experiential.* This is a high-impact or high-risk matter for the client. Such important work is going to go to the lawyer who the client feels will personally handle it. The client will find a limited number of lawyers qualified to perform the work. About 16 percent of the work available in a market is experiential.
3. *Brand Name.* This work is more routine but still important to the client. It is going to go to the firm or group of lawyers who have established a brand name with the client. Size is an important factor here, but reputation for a niche is just as important. About 20 percent of the work available in a market is brand name.
4. *Commodity.* In the view of clients, this is work that practically any good lawyer can perform. The majority of the work available in a market, about 60 percent, is commodity work and very price-sensitive.

Although these classifications appear precisely defined in Figure 3-1, there is in fact a transition range from one classification to another. The curve may differ slightly with different industries and different types of work and between businesses and individuals, but the principle is the same. Note how quickly the value of work tapers off in the market. Before the work gets to brand name, it is already becoming price-sensitive.

To get a quick feel for what these classifications mean, think of some calls the lawyer might receive from a significant business client about a legal problem:

♦ *Unique.* The CEO or chairman of the board calls.
♦ *Experiential.* The general counsel or a top-level executive calls.
♦ *Brand Name.* One of the assistant general counsels or a mid-level executive calls.
♦ *Commodity.* One of the department managers calls.

Applications of the Curve

The lawyer must assess the value of legal services he or she delivers relative to other lawyers in the market. An objective assessment will show that clients place matters, services, and legal products at different points on the value curve.

When a law firm or individual lawyer adequately assesses the markets in which it competes for delivering legal services, the value curve provides additional insights. Billing rates for a lawyer are driven by operating costs. These costs include the cost of occupancy, employees, investments in technology, and, of course, the required draws of the partners or minimum distributions to the lawyer. When the average billing rates due to leverage are overlaid on the value curve, the value of services may not coincide with the value to the client.

For example, Figure 3-2 shows the range of billing rates for Firm 1, which are driven by overhead and lawyer tenure. Even at the lowest billing rate, such a high-overhead firm cannot do much commodity work without significant write-downs or effective use of substantive systems. Firms with particular structures and overhead cannot, in the context of a competitive market, be all things to all clients. The lower operating costs for Firm 2 mean that the range of billing rates will be lower. Of course, if a firm uses only hours as the key element in evaluating its performance, instead of return on the hour (realization), then any work along the curve will be acceptable.

The value curve is the tool that can be used to analyze the firm's competitive position within a market. That market could be a geographic market, a client segment market (large commercial loan departments), a client, or an area of practice (environmental).

Figure 3-2   Position of Two Firms on the Value Curve

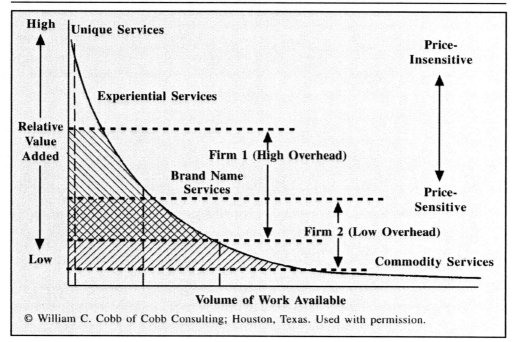

© William C. Cobb of Cobb Consulting; Houston, Texas. Used with permission.

Implications of the Curve
Competitive Position

A lawyer must understand his or her relative competitive position by service or bundles of services offered. A lawyer can move up the curve by improving intake procedures to focus on higher-value work. However, a very high-value service in the market in one month may move from point 1 to point 4 in Figure 3-3 as volume increases and as new competitors enter the market.

To maintain their competitive position and stop the slippage of value as more competitors enter the market, firms add value to the services offered. Sources of added value include timeliness, quarterly client briefings, project management, project status reporting, and other additions to the standard bundle of services.

Price

Where a client would locate a service on the value curve will determine what the client is willing to pay in either billing rates or some other form of fee. If a client wants a particularly stellar lawyer to appear in court on an experiential matter, the lawyer may be able to charge 150 percent, 200 percent, or even 500 percent of his or her normal billing rate. If the task is a commodity project, the

Figure 3-3   Sample Points on the Value Curve

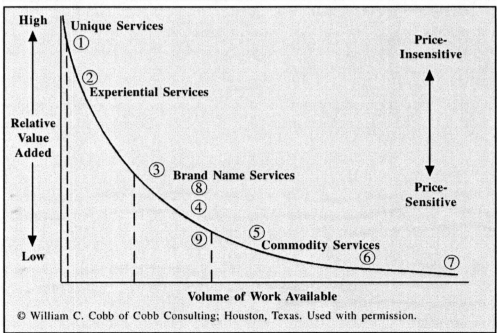

© William C. Cobb of Cobb Consulting; Houston, Texas. Used with permission.

client may want a very low billing rate or fixed fee. If the work is in the brand name range, the client may want the blended rate (the average billing rate per hour) for the work to be competitive.

The lawyer or firm must understand its relative competitive position as a provider of certain services. Within a firm, groups also may provide services to significant clients with specific ranges of value. The real estate group may be offering services that range from point 2 to point 4 in Figure 3-3. The securities group may be offering services that range from points 1 to 3. The litigation group may be offering services that range from points 3 to 6. Therefore, the pricing approaches of these groups may vary, and their structure and leverage also may vary.

The firm and lawyers must interview clients to determine their value system. Individual employees of the client may have different objectives, which also must be understood in the acceptance of any work. Always ask, "Who *is* the client?" One corporate officer may be trying to win quickly, another may be trying to postpone settlement, and still another may be trying to protect his or her corporate position by hiring the largest firm. Therefore, the added value of timeliness may be important to one and not another.

Realization is the percentage that the firm receives through collections on standard billing rates. If the standard billing rate for a lawyer is $150 per hour and the effective collected rate is $135 per hour, the total realization is 90 percent. Losing 1 percent of realization has the same effect on the bottom line as does writing off 1 percent of the hours worked or giving a discount of 1 percent on standard billing rates. If the lawyers' fees are above the client's value curve (e.g., point 8 in Figure 3), the lawyer will end up getting only the value the client perceives—point 4—and realization will therefore be less than 100 percent. If the lawyer's fees for the same project are normally at point 9 and the client has agreed in the engagement letter to pay the price reflected in point 4, realization will be greater than 100 percent. A 1 percent increase in realization produces the same increase to distributable income as a 1 percent increase in hours or standard rates.

Law Firm Structure

Firm structure and the leverage used by the firm must be driven by the types of services offered, *not by some arbitrary ratio.* A particular leverage ratio will not guarantee profitability. For example, a firm operating in a niche that is experiential and unique in the market may operate without much leverage and still maintain a high level of profitability. One of the reasons some New York firms are so profitable is that they are able to use leverage in the unique and experiential classifications of work.

If the firm is going to compete in the brand name area, it must have some leverage to lower the average billing rates so that they are competitive. Using only partner time in the brand name area will soon price the firm out of that market.

If the firm must compete in the commodity area, it must significantly leverage the work through delegation. The firm must also use substantive systems to minimize the number of professional hours used to create legal products.

Using the Value Curve

Using the value curve as a tool, determine the value to the client of each element, based upon the client's value system and price-sensitivity. Each element of work is a task or the development of a legal product. Assign each element of work an hourly rate, a blended rate, a fixed rate, a fixed price or flat fee, or a contingency fee:

- *Hourly billing rate.* Use this when you don't know the time for the element of work or the mix of professionals required. The hourly rate is the rate that appears on the work-in-process billing memorandum. If the total fee on the billing memorandum is $10,000 and the total number of hours in the matter is 100 hours, then the weighted average billing rate, or hourly rate, would be $100 per hour.

- *Blended billing rate.* Use this when you don't know the time for the element of work but can anticipate the mix of the professions to accomplish the task. For example, if a fixed rate quoted to the client is set at $135 per hour, the client is assured of a fixed rate for the task. Internally this was based on assumptions about who would be doing the work. For example, the $200 partner anticipates 25 percent of the time in the task, an associate at $125 will put in 50 percent of the time, and a paralegal at $75 will put in 25 percent of the time. Thus, the blended rate will be $131.25, providing a premium of $3.75 per hour. If the partner can manage the task more efficiently to get an additional 5 percent of the work to the associate, the blended rate in work in process will be $127.50, for another $3.75 premium. If the blended-rate tasks amount to 1,000 hours, the premium will be $7.50 times 1,000, or $7,500. The effective billing rate for each timekeeper will be 106 percent of standard. For example, the associate's effective billing rate will be $132.35 per hour. If, across the firm, the blended billing rate can be used for up to 10,000 hours each month, with no increase of overhead, the premium will increase. That premium will also replace many hours of billable time and allow the partners time for improving service and client relationships.

- *Fixed or flat fee.* Use such a fee when you can estimate the time for the effort and anticipate the mix of professionals. For example, the preparation of an employment agreement may be estimated for the client at a fee of $100. If the partner can create a system to produce the legal product at $75, each employment agreement will produce a premium of $25. The effective billing rate of the professionals working on the agreement will be 133 percent of their standard billing rate.

- *Contingency fee.* This is appropriate when you feel there is a bona fide cause of action and can afford to make the investment in the matter or case. Given enough time for negotiations with the client, use a reverse contingency. For example, if you and the client can agree that the probable legal expense will be $200,000 and you can dispose of the matter within 90 days, you may get 50 percent of the difference between your fees and the $200,000. This is a simple example, but lawyers throughout the country are using variations of this approach.

Once you have identified each phase, milestone, and element and have established the most appropriate pricing approach for each element, you can use the outline to budget the effort and assign appropriate professional resources.

The Value Curve for Main Street Lawyers

Many solo practitioners and small firm lawyers spend a larger portion, if not all, of their time representing individual consumers of legal services and local "mom and pop" businesses. The smaller business owner often has more in common with a consumer making any other type of purchasing decision than with the business-to-business analysis of the large law firm negotiating with the large corporate client.

The lessons in the use of the value curve hold true for the small town lawyers, suburban lawyers, and those in other practice settings who represent mainly consumers. Some of these lawyers consider themselves to be general practitioners, while others have highly specialized or limited practices, focusing on consumer bankruptcy, criminal defense, or family law as examples. Many lawyers in urban settings also have these types of practices. For easy reference and lack of a better term, let us refer to these lawyers collectively as the Main Street lawyers.

Commodity Work

Let us examine these classifications, starting with commodity work. Many Main Street lawyers will often find that their practices have far more than 60 percent commodity work, perhaps even approaching 100 percent. This should not be taken as a disparagement or belittlement. Nor should this fact suggest that these matters are unimportant. In fact, one can argue on several levels that a contested child custody determination is more important and profound than a dispute between two large corporations over a contract provision. As stated, this is the majority of work in the legal marketplace. There are certainly many associates in large law firms whose present workload consists of 100 percent commodity work.

Acknowledging the legitimacy of the value curve and its definition of commodity matters may answer some questions that have nagged at Main Street lawyers. Most of these lawyers have experienced some puzzling disappointments in the legal marketplace: a long-term client going to a new wet-behind-the-ears lawyer in town for no apparent reason, a client who discusses a matter with the lawyer in depth but then apparently takes no action, locals taking significant matters to firms in larger urban areas when local lawyers are more than competent to handle the work, otherwise reasonable and responsible clients disputing legal fees, and so forth.

Understand that the predominant market variable of commodity legal services is their extreme price-sensitivity. The lawyer's reputation and past services may well take a back seat to pricing factors in this sector. It is often difficult for the Main Street lawyer to accept this premise. When a lawyer has through herculean efforts rescued a family from the brink of disaster or obtained a financial settlement that changed a client's life, it is difficult to believe that a few years later this client may select another lawyer to draft his will based on a price savings of $50, but the value curve suggests how this can happen; indeed, many lawyers have experienced this precise event.

One situation particularly hard for the Main Street lawyer to digest and accept is the client who goes to a provider that the lawyer views as providing inferior services. The practitioner fresh out of law school may offer a significantly lower hourly billing rate, but the experienced lawyer "knows" that his expertise will allow him to accomplish the task much more quickly, resulting in the same or even a smaller total fee.

The price-sensitive consumer may, on the other hand, focus on only one comparison. The experienced lawyer is quoting an hourly rate of $165 per hour, while the rookie quotes an hourly rate of $90. This illustrates a pitfall of hourly rates in consumer commodity practice. The experienced lawyer may offer a better work product and superior advice. But the only information given to the client is an impression that the services costs nearly twice as much.

If the project was quoted on a flat-fee basis with both lawyers quoting a total fee of $450, what is the likely result then? The experienced lawyer with a past connection to the family will more than likely be retained over the new lawyer in town. This may well be true even if the experienced lawyer's price is slightly higher. But lawyers must remain attuned to the fact that we have reached an era in the legal profession where there is an extreme price-sensitivity in these types of matters.

With competition from do-it-yourself kits, Internet legal services, independent paralegals and other nonlawyer service providers, the conflict is even greater. The price differential may be even more extreme.

Quality looms as an issue, too. With the new lawyer in town, there was at least an expectation that the services would be done correctly—"practically any good lawyer" can do the commodity practice. Can the same be said of an untrained document preparer or an Internet document assembly service? In discussing with clients the preparation and execution of do-it-yourself documents, the Main Street lawyer may be able to recount many past problems resulting from documents incorrectly completed, never finished, or never filed. Courts are seeing more and more divorce pleadings, for example, that were provided over the Internet and fail to comply with that jurisdiction's requirements. While independent paralegals who provide services directly to consumers are licensed and recognized in a few states, many lay document drafters do not have the training and experience to recognize any pitfalls that a particular legal form might conceal. Objectively, it may be that the lawyer's service is superior in many ways beyond the document itself (e.g., the lawyer accepts potential liability for errors and has a stringent code of ethics). But in fairness it must be said that there may be times when a local, experienced paralegal can produce documents indistinguishable from those that the lawyer would have done.

While it may be somewhat humbling to accept, the value curve helps us understand that the nationally known lawyers who are often featured on television and have become household names, at least in legal circles, may still be able to name their price "take it or leave it" in the unique and experiential matters. But things are now different for many legal services widely believed to be routine.

Consumers themselves even use language that indicates they believe their work to be commodity work. ("I just want a simple will." "We do not have much." "This probably doesn't sound that important to you, but. . . .") There is certainly a tendency for many consumers to now believe that a will is a will, no matter who drafts it, or that the conclusion of a probate case is fairly preordained no matter who handles it for them.

The opportunity here is for lawyers to be armed with the appreciation of the price-sensitivity issue of commodity work and to craft an approach that is a win-win for both the lawyer and the client. This does not mean a price war of reckless underbidding that does not benefit the lawyer in the end. But it may mean highlighting the other values that the lawyer provides.

Brand Name

The brand name market grouping is readily recognized by Main Street lawyers, particularly those who practice in a small community. Certain lawyers may be recognized as preeminent within the legal community and perhaps within the broader community as well. There may be one firm that has several lawyers, while the other lawyers in the community operate either as solos or duos. In the community with only one or two banks, for example, many people know which lawyer represents the bank and sits in on its board meetings. While there may be many competent family practice lawyers in a community, there always seem to be a few who are often seen representing a party when a divorce or other legal problem strikes the community's most wealthy or influential citizens.

Other examples abound, from the second generation of lawyers representing the second or third generation of owners of a local business to the affluent citizen who wants the best of everything, including seeking out the "best" lawyer in town.

This is one area where the ultimate truth of the value curve applies, but the application is a bit more indirect. When viewing the legal market from a national or global perspective, there might seem to be fewer brand name service opportunities than the 20 percent that are projected. But within a given community, this percentage at least seems accurate. The prominent feature of this area of legal business is the client seeking out the lawyer based on reputation or perceived expertise. Lawyers hope that as they become more experienced, their practice will likewise mature by including an increasing number of these desirable attorney-client relationships.

Experiential and Unique

For the purposes of this discussion, we can combine the experiential (a high-impact or high-risk matter for the client, composing about 16 percent of the legal work) and the unique (the utmost importance or nuclear event, composing about 4 percent).

This combined category embraces all of the deadly serious, life-or-death needs for legal services. Hanging in the balance is the survival of the company, success or bankruptcy, the accomplishments of a lifetime, one's freedom of movement, or perhaps even one's very life. The client is focused. The stakes are enormous. It is understandable that the price of legal services recedes into the background here and the ultimate outcome holds center stage. This does not mean that there are no ethical, practical, or moral restraints on the fee that can be charged. As noted in Chapter Two, the fee must always be reasonable. The client's resources may be limited even though the motivation may be high.

It is useful, however, to understand the dynamics of this combined category. Indeed, there is one familiar group of lawyers who often represent clients who have problems of this magnitude and, generally speaking, constitute the group of lawyers most free from the dependence on hourly billing. An example of just such a group is the criminal defense bar.

Indeed, for most individuals a serious criminal charge is the nuclear event. Certainly the prospect of the destruction of one's reputation, imprisonment, and even the potential of the ultimate penalty is exceedingly serious. The ordeal of a criminal trial is so filled with conflict and drama that countless movies, television shows, and novels have been placed in this setting. There is no doubt that these cases involve large stakes.

Not any lawyer will do. Members of the public now generally understand that not all lawyers go to court and not all litigators handle criminal matters.

So how have the members of the bar who have served this clientele charged for their services? Generally speaking, criminal defense attorney's fees are not determined on an hourly rate. Instead, they are most often charged under the types of so-called alternative billing methods we have been discussing—either a flat fee for the entire defense or a set of clear landmarks (e.g., one fee for grand jury proceeding, another through preliminary hearing, and another for the jury trial). In most instances, the fees are payable in advance. We do understand that some white-collar criminal defense cases are still contracted on an hourly basis—but not often. There are several factors that lead to a flat fee or similar alternative method, with assurance of payment being one. If a defense is unsuccessful, it may be difficult to obtain payment. It seems self-evident that mailing billing statements to a prison cell is likely to be unsuccessful. There is an obligation among defense counsel to explore all avenues of defense, so this should neither be a situation where client and lawyer can make joint business decisions about the scope of the representation.

The point for the Main Street lawyer is that the Cobb Value Curve does predict the conclusion here. In the nuclear events, there is little price-sensitivity.

Major Issues Regarding Billing Methods

Pause here to think about some of the concepts that have been advanced to this point. As you read further, consider some of the major issues confronting the legal profession with respect to billing methods, such as the following:

- Is the now predominant method of hourly billing the best way to measure the value of legal services?
- How should value be measured?
- Is there any way by which value can be objectively measured?
- Who determines the value—the lawyer or the client—even if the test is to be the value to the client?

- Is the process truly a matter of value in the theoretical sense, or can it be accomplished on a workable, practical, day-to-day basis?
- Are there several different billing methods that can be used on a case-by-case method or in the same client matter that will measure value to the mutual benefit of lawyer and client?
- Is the ultimate issue how to utilize traditional and innovative billing methods in new ways to fit individual situations? In such a case, tailoring billing methods to fit different clients, phases, or matters may be the most precise approach.
- How can lawyers be educated to understand and accept the concept of alternative billing methods (including the problem of lawyer egos and "value")? Chapter 11 includes some possible approaches.
- How can you implement and control the use of alternative billing methods in a law firm with many partners? This problem is exacerbated as the firm grows more into an institutional style with multiple departments and offices.

Using Your Current Practice to Plan and Build a Billing Method

4

What billing system is right for my practice? How can I change from an hourly based billing system to a value based system? How do I determine if my practice can make such a change? These are all questions that must be asked and answered before a lawyer should consider changing billing methods. This chapter presents some checklists of some things you should do and some tools for you to use to determine the cost of producing your legal services and evaluating the billing method suitable for your particular practice.

Before starting any crossover from an hourly (cost-based) billing method to an alternative (value-based) method, you need to know your own environment and practice and to go through a detailed process of self-assessment.

Self-Assessment Checklist

The considerations described in Chapter Three relating to pricing legal services in your practice area and the effect of the value curve will strongly influence your choice of billing methods. Ask the following questions to help you focus and assess what your practice is all about and which billing methods are appropriate to help you reach your objectives.

Objectives and Goals

- ◆ The solo practitioner, firms of all sizes, and in-house counsel need to set objectives and goals. Do you have firm objectives and goals for your practice?
- ◆ What are your strengths and weaknesses?
- ◆ What opportunities exist in your market that you might not have addressed?
- ◆ What services do you now provide?
- ◆ What services should you provide in order to address market opportunities and meet your goals and objectives?
- ◆ How do you as owner(s) of the firm perceive your organization, its competitive advantages and disadvantages?
- ◆ Are your perceptions realistic and supported by the facts?
- ◆ How do your perceptions fit with your clients' perceptions? Prospective clients' perceptions? How will you find out?
- ◆ Who are your lawyers and staff, and what are their talents?
- ◆ What is the experience mix of your firm's lawyers, and how does it fit the needs of your clients and prospective clients?
- ◆ Who are your clients, and what are their legal needs now or in the foreseeable future?
- ◆ How do your firm's talents meet the needs of your clients?
- ◆ Do your clients believe that you or your firm has the skills to meet their needs as they perceive them?
- ◆ Do the services you provide your clients vary in where they fit on the value curve?
- ◆ Where does your practice fit on the value curve?
- ◆ Are there services you currently provide that should be dropped due to their place on the value curve?

Present and Future Market Trends

- ◆ What are the market trends?
- ◆ What is the demography of:
  - ◆ your firm?
  - ◆ your clients?
  - ◆ your legal community?
  - ◆ your community or market area?
- ◆ Who are your competitors, and where are they located?
- ◆ In what practice areas do they compete?
- ◆ What are the prevailing rates for the types of services you provide in your market, especially if you are providing services that are price-sensitive?

- Who are your clients?
- What are the needs of your present or potential clients?
- Do your current clients have legal needs that are presently being handled by other firms?
- Are these areas of practice that you are or should be providing?

Current Billing Methods

- Do your current billing methods enable you to achieve a desired level of profitability?
- Do your current billing methods meet client needs and preferences?
- Do they enable you to compete effectively?
- Do they enable you to further your firm's goals?
- Do they fairly measure value to the client?
- Are they consistent with trends?
- Do they promote effective marketing?
- Are they based on written fee agreements?
- Have they been innovative? flexible?
- Are your current billing methods different for different types of services?
- Are they competitive in your market area as to price?

Willingness to Try Innovative Billing

- Have you analyzed your practice to determine those practice areas or types of services for which alternative or innovative billing methods might be beneficial?
- Are you or some members of your firm willing to innovate?
- Do you have clients who have requested or might be willing to accept alternative billing methods?
- Are you willing to take the time and make the effort to bring about a change in how you bill for legal services?
- Will your firm support the effort?

Thoughtful consideration of the preceding questions can provide insight, and completing this preliminary self-assessment is an important first step. However, it is not enough to merely mentally review these questions. As with any project, some written notes add a framework and aid in the retention of any thoughts and observations. Actually providing writing materials to the lawyer or lawyers analyzing these inquiries is clearly useful, if not required. The lawyer must weigh the pros and cons to determine whether the environment is such that innovation in billing has a chance to succeed or in what areas it has the best chance to succeed initially.

Only then are you ready for the next step: determining the cost of producing the legal services.

Determining Cost

Budgeting, cost tracking, and other accounting aspects of the practice of law are often ignored by the lawyers in large firm settings and can easily be over-looked or not addressed at all in the solo or small firm setting. The larger firm may have a "back office" department that handles all billing and accounting operations, both for money and attorney's time, but the average lawyer in the large firm has little to do with those functions. The smaller firm may have an administrator or office manager, but that person may have a variety of time-consuming duties to juggle. In practices of all sizes, monthly financial tracking and reporting will often be pushed aside by the more urgent need to address client projects or prepare accurate and complete billing statements for clients. Budgets and costs are often just lost in the shuffle.

Many lawyers dislike the business aspects of law practice and are content not to deal with too many financial reports. So if the net income after paying expenses is sufficient for the lawyer's needs, little attention may be paid to the specifics. The balance of this chapter covers areas often ignored by lawyers in their practice, but necessary to properly determine what the best billing method might be for a particular type of work or project. Costs must be understood and addressed by the lawyer before billing methods (even hourly billing) can be selected as appropriate for the task.

For the purposes of planning for alternative billing, costs of legal services can be roughly divided into two categories:

1. the fixed or overhead expenses that may be fairly constant; and
2. the costs incurred in providing the actual services (the time invested) and direct cost associated with those services.

This chapter deals with both analyzing a practice and determining a suitable billing method.

Retrospective Analysis of Cost as a Guide

Few law offices formally base individual billing rates exclusively on costs. Rather, the new associate billing rate is often set by using the "rule of three" (salary times three, divided by the minimum required billable hours, equals billing rate) or some modification thereof. Other timekeeper rates are usually based on some percentage increase over last year, what each partner thinks about his or her own rate, and some "Kentucky windage" based on what is heard on the street or from clients, and what is known about the rates other firms charge for similar services or years of experience.

Cash collections are then estimated based on hours to be worked and cash collection percentages. Estimated costs are deducted. And if resulting profits are reasonably acceptable, rates are adopted.

The good news is that this approach has worked in the past. The bad news is that it does not work as well today and will work less well in the future for several reasons:

- ◆ Not all costs of doing business are usually tracked. Those that are omitted may include rate adjustments to client bills, money costs, partner costs, and event costs.
- ◆ Individual client or matter profitability is difficult to determine with this approach.
- ◆ Costs are not matched with related revenues.
- ◆ Utilization and leverage cost differences are not highlighted at the matter level.
- ◆ Client value isn't anywhere to be seen (unless there is a problem).

What is needed to guide the billing process is a much broadened view. That view should include all items affecting the cost of providing a service to a client, the value to the client, as well as the economics of supply and demand.

Cost of Service Versus Value to the Client

As discussed earlier, value is determined by the buyer of the service and may have little relation to the cost of the service. For example, at the high end of the value curve, there is essentially no relationship of value to cost. At the low end, value and cost are almost synonymous, or the cost of the service may actually exceed the value to the client. In between these two points on the value curve, the cost/value relationship varies depending on where you are on the curve, as shown in Figure 4-1 on page 38.

> Note that no billing amount for a particular service has yet been set. The billing amount is (or should be) dependent on the cost of providing a service, as well as on the lawyer's skill in demonstrating value in the eyes of the client and his or her willingness or desire to bill that amount. This is what converts the billing process from a mechanical step to an "art." It is what is often lacking in a straight hourly billing method.

Figure 4.1   Value/Cost Curves in the Legal Profession

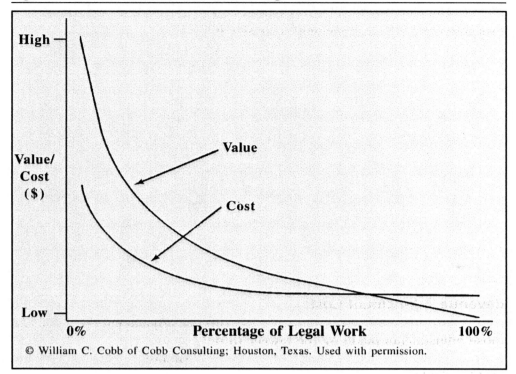

© William C. Cobb of Cobb Consulting; Houston, Texas. Used with permission.

Knowing Costs Through Accounting

Cost accounting dates back to the late 1800s and has its roots in the manufacturing industries. Only in the last few decades has this concept been applied to the service industries and, more recently, to the legal profession. The reason for this delayed application is, basically, that it was not needed. As long as lawyers could increase hourly rates with little resistance from clients, the cost of delivering legal services was not very important. This has changed, and more and more law offices are finding that understanding what it costs to deliver legal services is essential for managing profitability.

The repetitive themes that emerge when law offices start thinking about using cost accounting techniques are the KISS (Keep It Simple, Stupid) principle and fear of divisiveness. This book does not deal with the fear of divisiveness or profitability management, nor does it get into the specifics of cost accounting. However, it will be helpful to review cost accounting from the KISS viewpoint.

Costs

Most matters involve five different types of costs. In the format of a profit-and-loss statement, they are accounted for as follows:

Revenue	$XXX
Revenue adjustment costs	XX
Net revenue	$XXX
Timekeeper costs	$ XX
Overhead (indirect) costs	XX
Event (support) costs	XX
Money costs	XX
Total costs	$ XX
Net profit	$ XX

At the matter or case level, each of these costs can be determined as described in the following discussion.

Revenue Adjustment Costs

For purposes of this discussion, the term "revenue adjustment costs" means those adjustments made by the lawyer to billings—either before (rate and billing adjustments or write-ups and write-downs) or after (write-offs) bills are sent to clients. There are three types of revenue adjustment costs:

1. *Rate adjustments.* These relate to the difference between the "value" of timekeepers' time (based on time spent and "standard" hourly rates) and the value based on front-end agreements made with the client as to hourly rate adjustment or other fee determination agreements. Rate adjustments can be either premiums (for additional value) or discounts (for any number of business reasons, including the desire to be in a new market or to obtain a new client).

2. *Billing adjustments.* These relate to the difference between an agreed-upon billing amount (hourly rate, premium, discount, etc.) and the amount billed to the client. Such adjustments may be due to inefficiencies or efficiencies that are not passed on to the client.

3. *Write-offs.* Typically these are adjustments to billed amounts when a client objects to a portion of the bill or for bad debts.

Timekeeper Costs

Timekeeper costs are the direct costs of individuals serving clients on a particular matter. At the level of the firm, office, and department (or practice group), these costs are the actual costs incurred during the period. At the level of matter (and area of law), client (SIC code, location, client type), or billing lawyer, these costs should be determined on the basis of "standard" hourly direct and indirect cost rates and would generally include an imputed cost for partners.

Overhead Costs

The firm's overhead costs are the various indirect costs associated with keeping open the doors of the law office: support staff, rent, supplies, depreciation, continuing education, and so on.

Event Costs

Event costs include the cost of nontimekeeper services provided directly to a matter. These include such internal services as document creation, copying, computerized research, and long-distance telephone charges.

Money Costs

Money costs represent the cost of borrowed funds or partner capital related to the investments made in a matter from the time incurred until ultimately collected. Such investments may be timekeeper, overhead, and event costs plus out-of-pocket costs paid by the firm.

A Simple Exercise in Cost Accounting

Someone already trained in elementary accounting usually spends about one quarter in college learning cost accounting. While a cost accounting analysis would be far more complete starting at the firm and practice group level, an individual lawyer in a larger firm or in a solo or small firm practice doesn't need that in determining his or her costs. This section is designed to provide a simple exercise for a lawyer or a small firm or practice group to use to determine a basic measure of his or her costs in delivering service.

Overhead Costs

The overhead costs are a portion of all other operating costs of the law office. Overhead is allocated to the lawyer on the basis of timekeeper weighting factors. Thus, more overhead costs typically would be assigned to partners than to associates, and to associates more than to legal assistants. Determining weighting factors is particular to the practice group or firm. It is pretty simple in a small firm or solo practice.

Event Costs

Event costs are generally charged to the matters directly based on estimated or actual use of usage-type resources (word processing, long-distance telephone service, copying, and computerized legal research). These can often be tracked within the firm's billing system.

Money Costs

To calculate money costs, multiply the following factors:

The investment in unbilled work and costs plus the billed but uncollected fees and costs of the billing lawyers assigned to the practice group.	X	The interest rate the firm pays on bank loans.

Revenue Adjustment Costs

Revenue adjustment costs are the revenue adjustments recognized for each matter. Some billing or client accounting systems may not track rate adjustments. If not, they can be easily calculated for each matter by tracking specific rate or billing adjustments and write-offs.

Timekeeper and Overhead Costs

To find timekeeper and overhead costs, multiply the hours charged to the matter by standard timekeeper and overhead hourly cost rates. To determine those rates, divide actual timekeeper costs and indirect costs allocated to each timekeeper (category) by the timekeeper's chargeable hours. If a timekeeper has significant amounts of nonchargeable management or firm time, add the cost of these hours to indirect costs, and use total chargeable and nonchargeable hours as the divisor in determining the timekeeper's hourly cost rate.

Determining Cost to Produce a Package of Services

Using the information just given, you can determine the cost of providing a service and its net profit. The following example shows how for a small two-attorney firm.

Revenue	
Standard value of hours (hours times hourly standard rates)	
Partner A (160 × $200)	$32,000
Associate B (80 × $150)	12,000
Revenue adjustments	
Rate adjustments (160 x $20)	3,200
Billing adjustments (5%)	(2,360)
Write-offs	0
Net revenue	$44,840

Costs

Service Provider

Direct:	Partner A (160 x $88)		$14,080
	Associate B (80 x $50)		4,000
Overhead:	Partner A (160 x $97)		15,520
	Associate B (80 x $61)		4,880
Support (events) (5 hours x $20)			100
Money (assume 6 months to pay)			2,240
	Total costs		$40,820
	Net profit		$ 4,020

Calculate costs per hour for the timekeepers as follows:

	Partner A	**Associate B**
Imputed or actual annual compensation and fringe benefits	$150,000	$ 90,000
Allocation of annual overhead	$165,000	$110,000
Budgeted hours	1,700	1,800
Costs per hour		
Compensation (direct)	$ 88	$ 50
Overhead (indirect)	$ 97	$ 61

Task-Based Analysis

All professionals struggle with answering the client's question of how much a service will cost. The usual answer is, "I don't know because I don't know how much time it will take. I don't know how the other side will respond. I can't tell how much research is required. I can't predict how you will respond to alternatives. . . ."

Although this answer may be correct, the client may still insist on receiving a ballpark estimate or on knowing whether the case size is of breadbox or elephant proportions. The way to solve this problem is to use solutions based on techniques used in business and government for fifty years called CPM (Critical Path Method) and PERT (Program Evaluation and Review Technique). These two systems use the following procedure to analyze projects:

◆ Segment projects into tasks and related subtasks.
◆ Estimate resources required to complete each subtask.
◆ Estimate the time or cost of each resource.
◆ Identify the interdependent relationships of tasks and subtasks.
◆ Estimate the likely variability of each resource requirement and time estimate.

If a litigation lawyer follows these steps, he or she will find that many, if not all, cases can easily be segmented into tasks such as these:

- ◆ Issue identification.
- ◆ Discovery.
- ◆ Trial preparation.
- ◆ Trial.
- ◆ Appeal.

Further, each of these tasks can be segmented into subtasks. Transaction lawyers can segment transactions the same way.

When using these techniques, you will find that you can estimate the resource and time requirements with more certainty (less variability) for early tasks than for later tasks. However, this should not prevent you from making reasonably educated estimates of ranges of resource and time requirements, with, of course, more uncertainty (broader ranges) for each succeeding task. By way of example, it is easier to estimate resources for the earlier stages of a piece of litigation, such as issue identification and discovery, than for later stages, such as trial preparation and trial, since what is required in each stage is often a function of what was learned in the previous one.

This type of task plan is particularly valuable in discussing case variables and their likely cost impacts with clients. It also can help you to begin communicating the value of the various tasks to the overall matter.

Examining Closed Files to Create Minisystems and Predict Fees

Experience is the best tool for predicting fees. A lawyer's experience in dealing with different problems can be found in closed files and billings, which offer a treasure trove of information on how long certain procedures might take and what resources might be devoted to them. When trying to predict the future, as one does when estimating costs, a good approach is to know what has happened in the past. This means knowing what resources were required in similar prior cases. There are two methods for doing this:

1. Examine closed files and billings.
2. Begin documenting experience on current cases by modifying current timekeeping systems so that you can segment matters into tasks and subtasks.

Examining prior files and bills will help you identify tasks and subtasks as well as time requirements and reasons for variability. Your closed files and old billing records can be an invaluable resource to mine for establishing the costs of delivering legal services.

Examine closed files and bills to determine how much time it took or what it cost the firm to perform the work involved. To get information about the average cost of production, group files and bills that involved repetitious work. This exercise can help you predict what you should try to charge. It may also show that you have been inefficient because you did not have a "case plan," a topic that will be discussed in Chapter Six. It may also point you in the direction of creating minisystems, making greater use of technology, or taking other steps that will increase productivity.

In your review of closed files and bills, you may discover that with certain types of services there are recurring "uncertainties" or variables. Although the variables may differ slightly from matter to matter, if you can determine the typical range of time required to deal with the variables, you can factor that into your fees. Using the simple estate-planning example, you may find that the cost of preparing the documentation was fairly constant from matter to matter, but the two major variables were (1) the time spent in the initial phase (conferring with the clients, gathering basic facts, and helping the clients decide what they wanted), and (2) revising documentation because the clients changed their minds about the terms of the wills you were asked to prepare. This approach is sometimes referred to as "cost pricing" (fixed plus variable plus profit). You may determine that the documents themselves can be charged at a fixed fee but that the conferences and analysis should be based on an hourly rate.

Documenting current experience will help you fine-tune the knowledge gained from examining closed files and bills and will provide a monitoring capability that you can use to test the validity of estimates made on new matters. This experience can then allow you to develop and maintain templates for different types of matters, not only to estimate costs (and profitability), but also to help convey value to the client.

Recurring Variables or Uncertainties

It has been said that one cannot predict the future, but one can shape the future by planning. Variables and uncertainties are what make predictions difficult (sometimes impossible). They do so because we cannot always identify all variables or uncertainties.

However, there are common variables and uncertainties that professionals learn about as they gain experience. Lawyers quickly learn that some of these are under their control and others are not. Each professional should develop his or her own list. Here are some to use as a starting point:

- ◆ Variables or uncertainties under the professional's control:
  - ◆ Effectiveness of negotiating fee and payment arrangements.
  - ◆ Methods used to define the "problem."
  - ◆ View as to the necessity for a "Cadillac" solution or commercially acceptable solution.
  - ◆ Type of resources required to develop a solution.
  - ◆ Resources previously developed in similar matters.
  - ◆ Priority placed on matter solution.
  - ◆ Effectiveness of resource supervision.
  - ◆ Quality of resources used.
  - ◆ Diligence in timely billing and collection follow-up.
- ◆ Variables or uncertainties not under the professional's control:
  - ◆ Client's view of desired solution.
  - ◆ Client reactions.
  - ◆ Actions of opposing counsel.
  - ◆ Court actions.
  - ◆ Resource availability and performance.
  - ◆ New, conflicting demands affecting priorities.
  - ◆ New facts and circumstances.
  - ◆ Acts of God.

Once you have developed a fairly comprehensive list of variables, you can start estimating the ranges of impact the identified variables are likely to have on the resources and time required to complete the various tasks and subtasks.

Also keep in mind that you need "cushions" to minimize the impact of incorrect estimates or unpredictable events.

Examining Profitability as It Relates to Billing

In all businesses, profitability depends on a relatively few key variables:

- ◆ Supply and demand.
- ◆ Product or service quality.
- ◆ Cost of resources.
- ◆ Productivity of resources and management (effectiveness/efficiency).
- ◆ Pricing strategies and effectiveness.

Assume for the moment that all the variables except for pricing strategies and effectiveness are constant. In such a case, profits depend on the pricing strategies used. Ultimately, of course, a firm's revenues and expenses—

and hence its profits, actual or desired—depend on the risks or opportunities associated with the uncertainties of the other variables listed. Therefore, one way to look at pricing strategies (billing decisions) is in light of the various risks and opportunities involved. Here are some examples:

- There is a great deal of price elasticity (flexibility in the price range) if you are the only lawyer in town (or in the country) with a reputation for producing a certain result. Thus, you might generate a great deal of profit by billing "what the traffic will bear."
- If the external factors affecting lawyer time requirements are quite variable, this suggests billing at competitive hourly rates.
- When internal factors are substantially variable but controllable, this suggests billing at a fixed fee for the service.
- Low demand for a service may suggest a contingent fee arrangement.
- A combination of these factors may suggest different billing arrangements for different segments of a matter or for different matters for the same client.

If you have good knowledge of the resources required for and the risks and opportunities associated with a particular matter, it will help you test or model the ways different billing arrangements will affect the bottom line. Then you can identify an appropriate billing method and assess the economic desirability of accepting a particular representation. One example might be in the estate planning area, where an analysis of the different types of plans allows you to charge a fixed fee for certain types of plan documentation but an hourly rate for consultations and other types of work for which you have less control over the time needed to do the work. Another example might be a corporate practice, where the fees can be fixed for a simple incorporation because of systems developed to prepare the documentation, but a different billing method—based upon the amount of negotiation required and the number of parties involved—is used for client consultations and drafting of employment and shareholder agreements.

Even if you are crossing over from a cost-based to a value-based billing philosophy, it is important to know your cost. If your cost of production exceeds the value to the client and therefore what you can collect, you will be unprofitable. To offset that problem, you will need to make one or more of the following changes:

- Reduce the cost of production to less than the price or value of the services.
- Enhance the value of your services to meet the client's perception of value, thus raising the price above the cost of production.
- Increase productivity by using technology or systems without increasing the cost of production.

◆ Failing this, eliminate a practice area, department, office, or type of work.

Factors for the Main Street Lawyer

Building Billing Methods for Main Street Lawyers

Consumer clients represent the most price-sensitive area of legal practice. Although there are a variety of reasons for this, one factor that cannot be ignored is the rise of advertisements quoting fees for many "standard" or "uncontested" legal services. Few communities seem to be exempt from this circumstance.

These consumer areas also receive some of the highest incursion by non-lawyer providers that offer document drafting services for matters like bankruptcy and uncontested divorce. These areas also harbor much confusion, because many of these clients seek simple solutions and "uncontested" fee structures when in fact they have a myriad of complicated problems.

The Main Street lawyer cannot ignore the effect of these market forces and attitudes. The lawyer must be prepared to differentiate the services he provides from those offered by others. The lawyer understands that the main advantage he offers is professionalism and the ultimate quality of the services. Clients are better served (and more likely persuaded to hire the lawyer) by being given concrete examples of the value a lawyer provides. Among these examples are attorney-client confidentiality, the lawyer's familiarity with the case when the uncontested matter becomes contested, the lawyer's years of training and experience, the time the client saves by having the lawyer provide services rather than using the "do it yourself" approach, and the lawyer's ability to appear in court and speak on behalf of the client (as many clients have a great fear of public speaking).

Even in a price-sensitive area, the lawyer cannot and should not attempt to compete on price alone. The concept of value includes paying a bit more to receive superior services or a superior result.

Dealing with Unsophisticated Clients

In consumer-oriented practices, lawyers deal with a greater percentage of relatively unsophisticated clients. This does not imply that these clients are in any way graceless or ignorant. But they are often inexperienced in dealing with attorneys. Whether the matter is adoption or arrest, wills or worker's compensation, the simple fact is that this client may never have needed a lawyer before and has no prior experience with the subject matter of the legal situation.

Therefore, some of the techniques discussed in this book simply cannot apply in the same way in this situation. There can be no give-and-take discussion about a choice between various alternative billing methods when the client has little or no understanding of the process. There is little common ground for negotiation, and the fee is often presented to the client as a take-it-or-leave-it proposition. For consumer legal services, fees are often based upon market forces and lawyer experience, rather than negotiation with prospective clients. In fact, many Main Street lawyers have a long tradition of refusing to negotiate their fees. This is understandable, particularly with hourly rates: a lawyer charges a set fee per hour, and it seems unfair to charge a lower rate to one client just because that client pleads for one. Also, many offices have been organized to compute at one rate, and instituting various billing rates would increase administrative complexity in preparing bills.

Most of us understand that a Main Street lawyer might offer a discount rate. But that rate would be reserved for business clients who had a regular volume of matters to be handled and could be counted on to always pay their bills, or perhaps it would be described as a "professional discount" given to those who are likely to refer new clients in the future. If there a discounted rate was available, it was for wholesale or preferred customers, while the client coming in off the street with a first-time need for a lawyer on a single matter—that was retail.

There have been ample ethical rules and community standards that prescribed a fairly narrow range for an acceptable fee or rate. Unsophisticated clients are those who might most appreciate the simplicity and clarity of many fixed-fee arrangements.

Suppose a potential client makes an appointment with a Main Street lawyer about a relatively straightforward probate proceeding. The lawyer will discuss the handling of the matter and disclose his or her billing rate. Many consumer clients will find that this hourly rate is not sufficient information. So almost immediately the question arises, "How many hours will it take?" or "What will the total cost be?" It is there that the legal profession often gives a most unsatisfactory answer: "It depends." There are many variables, some of which are still unknown. The lawyer can only state a broad range of possible high and low figures, with many disclaimers.

It is not surprising that this can be a source of frustration for the potential client. After all, most consumer purchasing experiences do not proceed like this. In retail stores, price tags and signs abound. Prices are stated in advance. Can one imagine buying a refrigerator after being told that the final price will be set only after the consumer has agreed to make the purchase? Even a car dealer will make a firm offer. The Main Street lawyer has a fairly accurate sense of what an average fee for the consumer client's matter will total. But the lawyer cannot give an exact quote when the number of total hours to be expended are unknown to the lawyer as well as the client.

Although some might see this reluctance as an attempt to conceal something from the consumer, in reality the lawyer is exercising time-tested judgment. The experienced lawyer knows that if an average fee is mentioned, the client will focus on that number as "the fee." If a lawyer quotes an estimated fee of $2,000, a final total billing of $2,165 may seem to the lawyer to be right on target. But too many clients will respond with "No, wait, you said $2,000." So the lawyer has learned to express the estimate as a range, with plenty of room at the top end to ensure that the total fee will almost certainly be less than the highest number mentioned. In this example, the lawyer, if pressed, will quote a range from a low of $2,000 to a high of $4,000 or $5,000.

How much more consumer friendly and nonthreatening this transaction would be if the lawyer would simply say, "This probate case can all be yours for the low price of $2,450!" We are all consumers. We understand the attraction of simplicity. We understand the value of limiting the risk of a charge being much higher than anticipated. It is disingenuous to deny that if we were the client, we would prefer the certainty of the fixed fee.

"Wait," the lawyers would cry. "There are many variables, many contingencies." The total legal services required are often outside the lawyer's control. An unreasonable opposing counsel, a procrastinating opposing party, or a recalcitrant judge can increase the workload by several orders of magnitude. The lawyer does not want to bear that risk, and the hourly rate serves that purpose well. Whether it is a necessary party who cannot be located for service of process or an unanticipated and complicated factual situation, if the matter becomes more burdensome, the lawyer who invests more time should be paid more.

But the lawyer does know the variables—far better than the client. In many ways, the lawyer doesn't want to get pinned down. The client will certainly be treated fairly, but the lawyer wants to avoid being treated unfairly himself by being forced to work many more hours without additional compensation.

In fact, in matters where significant contingencies might dramatically change the work involved, the fee arrangement need not be based on just one flat fee. The fee agreement may cover numerous contingencies: If event A happens, one fee will be charged. If B happens, then another fee. The most important thing is for the unsophisticated client to understand and comprehend fees quoted in this manner without referring to an hourly billing rate. They should no longer have to ask, "How many hours will it take?"

Where the sophisticated and experienced business client may need a jointly developed plan based on the experiences of both the client and the lawyer, the consumer client needs information, explanation, and less uncertainty about the future. Written materials for the client to take home and review are extremely useful in these situations.

We will discuss developing case or transaction plans in much more detail in Chapter Six, but for many consumer cases, so-called alternative pricing is quite naturally part and parcel of the case plan. The large law firm may invest in discussing costs or pricing structures with sophisticated clients, and those clients may choose à la carte from a set of possible services. Consumer clients, however, usually need their matters handled by one lawyer from beginning to end. These clients need understanding and reassurance, and they need certainty and as much information as possible about the uncharted waters ahead. Hourly billing may be simple for the lawyer, but a consumer will appreciate the clarity and certainty of a fixed fee—even if that certainty is embodied in a road map with a dozen different possible total fees, depending on future variables.

The Pricing Structure Can Form the Basis of the Office System

The pricing structure, when properly communicated to the client, can provide the basis of the attorney-client agreement and the case plan. The less familiarity the client has with the situation, the more detailed the disclosure should be.

So in the probate case example, the clients may indicate that they will probably hire the Main Street lawyer and ask about fees. In response, the lawyer produces not an intimidating document entitled Attorney Client Fee Agreement, but a document called a Case Plan. This document takes the form of a time line and may be more graphically designed than the standard legal document. After giving everyone concerned a copy, the lawyer traces the anticipated chain of events: drafting and filing documents, sending notices, and so on. At each stage in the proceeding, the document clearly notes what the attorney fees are at that stage. Much of this form can be preprinted, but there may be variables that will be determined by the client, such as sales of property within the probate. So there may be blanks on this form that will be completed during the interview.

There may be unknowns and unknowables, in which case the lawyer will make a good faith estimate *in writing*. But the end result will be a complete document detailing the entire course of the legal matter, the anticipated timing of events, a likely date of conclusion, an estimated attorney fee, and generally the maximum likely fee. This is not to say that this document or set of documents does not include many typical provisions and disclaimers.

Some lawyers will object to attaching any estimate at all to an unpredictable fee. They may also disagree with giving clients timelines for the completion of tasks, no matter how general. After all, probates do sometimes drag on. But the message to the client should be that they do not drag on in *this* lawyer's office. The beauty of the case plan is that it is constructed to interlock with the lawyer's office procedures. The case plan gives the lawyer's staff as well the client a road map of the anticipated tasks and timelines. The law firm's system provides not only for the drafting of required documents, but for important standardized client communications. In place of two-sentence transmittal letters, the client receives detailed status reports accompanying the file-stamped copies that make reference to events outlined in the case plan. When contingencies occur that trigger a fee increase, the system generates a thoughtful explanation and discussion of what has transpired to accompany the request for additional fees. The client has a reference guide throughout the matter to judge the lawyer's performance against predictions.

With this approach, the Main Street lawyer is highly motivated to improve, embellish, and streamline the system. Compared with other clients, the clients of the Main Street lawyer may get superior and regular detailed communications, since the lawyer has judged that a few "extra" letters are less expensive to the firm than receiving numerous "extra" telephone calls from the client.

And what of the estimate of the unknowable fee when the fee was underestimated due to an event that has now improbably occurred? Will the lawyer be judged by his own candor? ("Yes, I stated probably no more $2,000 and the charges are now $3,500. But, ...") This is yet another aspect of the system that the lawyer should design and prepare in advance. When it becomes evident that an estimated charge may be exceeded, a letter of explanation can be sent to the client immediately, not when the final fees are requested. ("Please be advised A and B have occurred, and the costs are exceeding our original estimate. You may contact me at no additional charge if you wish to discuss this.") This is not to say there will never be a time when a consumer manages to use a fee estimate against a lawyer, even if only for bargaining position to compromise the final fee. But the system functions to create understanding, predictability, and trust. A client is predisposed to view a contingency as something that has happened in his or her particular case, not as the lawyer simply deciding to charge more.

The benefit for the Main Street lawyer lies in having a system that encourages and rewards efficiency. Exploring advanced document assembly methods holds no downside. If the lawyer notes that he or she typically receives a number of calls at a particular stage in the representation, for which no additional compensation is received, the lawyer is motivated to improve communications in that area proactively, perhaps by covering the area better in the initial interview or by adding to the language contained in a standard client communication during this time frame. The Main Street lawyer constantly hones and improves the system, while the clients benefit from an ever-evolving model of client service, explanation, and communication.

I Cannot Do It at That Rate and Make Any Money

Often, the Main Street lawyer's initial reaction to decreasing fees in some consumer areas is steadfast insistence that lower fees make it impossible to turn a profit or to deliver competent representation. It is absolutely true that an in-depth examination of office procedures and the tasks to be accomplished on behalf of clients may drive the lawyer to the conclusion that certain practice areas are unprofitable and should be dropped. It may also be true that to be a full-service law firm for consumer clients, a small firm in a small community may have to handle some matters that are only marginally profitable.

But a Main Street lawyer cannot wish away market forces, the impact of information technology on the practice, or consumer attitudes. The simple fact is that many law offices have not arranged their operations for maximum efficiency. A lawyer may believe that a certain matter cannot be profitable based on the fact that it requires at least ten hours of lawyer time. But by fine-tuning and improving the system, the amount of lawyer time may be drastically reduced. The lawyer can use technology-based systems and/or support staff to leverage into a more profitable position. Some so-called routine legal services may be done for less and still be profitable. And the lawyer will then have more time available to work on other matters.

Conclusion

Now you are ready to try some cost accounting to determine the cost of production to be used as a guide in billing. Consider the advantage of knowing your cost of production broken down as follows (remember that you are seeking your cost, not the fee to be charged):

- By firm.
- By lawyer.
- By practice area.
- By department.
- By office (if you have more than one).
- By staff other than paralegals (fee chargers).
- By paralegals (fee chargers).
- By the use of technology (word processing, computers, etc.).
- By designated matter (or package of services).

In making your analysis, be on the lookout for groups of related services that you might package and be able to define in a "scope of the engagement" letter. For example, in estate planning, you might include initial conferences with the client, preparation of a will, trust agreement, durable and medical powers of attorney, living will, and a conference for execution of the documents. This exercise will help you learn whether you made a profit on those services (which you can use the next time you enter into a written fee agreement), and whether it would be possible to enter into a fixed or flat fee for that package of services.

A useful technique for determining fees for services that are easily packaged and normally recurrent is to keep track of the time spent in a number of representations. At the outset, write down your estimate of the minimum and maximum number of hours that will be expended to provide a defined service or package of services. Keep careful track of the actual time spent, and then compare the actual with the estimated time. See whether the actual time falls within the estimated minimum and maximum times.

After a number of such exercises, you will know whether you are a realistic estimator. Averaging the actual time spent in doing the same defined services for a number of clients, or repetitively for the same client, will give you a realistic basis for setting fees using any billing method. If you are considering billing on an hourly basis, you will have a sound basis for setting the hourly rate and giving a range of charges to your client. If you contemplate billing on a fixed-fee basis, this exercise will help you know whether the fixed fee will be satisfactory to you. If you work for a contingent fee, you will know whether that kind of work is profitable.

This exercise will not tell you whether your charges will be acceptable in the competitive marketplace, nor will it necessarily reflect the actual or perceived value of those services.

Although profitability is not the major focus of this chapter, the analysis that you make will enable you to determine the profitability of certain types of work. This information will be useful and may raise the following questions:

◆ On matters with low profit, can you increase volume enough or apply technology or other forms of leverage to make it desirable to continue that type of work?

◆ Was low profitability the result of strong competition?

◆ Was low profitability the result of your inefficiency, and can inefficiencies be reduced?

◆ Was low profitability due to inappropriate staff mix, and can that be adjusted?

◆ Can you justify low-profit work because it will enable you to get or keep high-profit work? (This is called a "loss leader.")

◆ Did you purposely set your fee low and with low profitability in order to enter a new market? (This is called "penetration pricing" and is designed to enable you to win market share.)

Technology and Alternative Billing

5

Technology affects the way lawyers produce their work and therefore affects their billing practices for producing that work.

No one can ignore the fact that law office technology has greatly changed the practice of law within the last two decades. Computers on lawyer's desks, automated document-drafting procedures, computerized legal research, handheld computers, easy access to the Internet, and dozens of other changes have affected both the way lawyers work and the actual nature of what is considered legal work within substantive areas of the practice of law.

Law office technology has revolutionized the practice of law, and as with most revolutions, there has been some degree of bloodshed. The implementation of technology within the law office is perhaps the greatest present force for change that affects the lawyer's business operations and opportunities for alternative methods of billing.

Lawyers have long used checklists, forms, brief banks, and other methods of reusing work products while enhancing and developing improved documents. It is probably fair to say at this point that no law office can reasonably function without using computers at least for word processing and the reuse of prior work products. By developing smart systems to expedite document production, lawyers reduce costs of production. This can yield benefits for the law firm or the client or both.

Technology can be the proverbial two-edged sword for the lawyer. Technology can provide relief from much mundane and repetitive work, shorten the time to complete tasks involving word processing, and allow a much more error-free final result. However, for the lawyer who bills by the hour, the use of technology can reduce the time expended on a project, which often equates to reduced fees.

In a traditional law firm structure, where an experienced partner might be able to do a certain task in far less time than the new associate, the difference was noted by the partner having a higher hourly billing rate. But as technological sophistication increases in legal business operations, it seems unlikely that the billing rate could be raised high enough to cover future contingencies. One can easily foresee a future where the law firm invests huge amounts of time and money in certain processes, with the end result being that the actual tasks take only seconds. It is no longer science fiction to envision a future where the lawyer first says to his computer, "Start with will form 6, insert Mr. Toffler's personal data into it, incorporate special tax treatments A and D, and show it being executed here today instead of in his home state," and then reaches for the completed documents as they instantly appear.

There is a very positive side to implementing improvements in law office technology. These tools can free lawyers and their staff from many mundane repetitive tasks. Efficiency can be increased. Given the complexity of the law today and the length of many legal documents, having technology to assist with document preparation and other tasks is an absolute necessity. E-mail saves time and money for law firms as well as their clients.

Another positive aspect of technology is the potential superior service that can be rendered to clients. Not only can digital legal research be done more quickly than the traditional review of books in a library, it can also be done more extensively. A couple of hours in the library might have allowed the traditional researcher to read a dozen recent opinions and a few more often-cited landmark opinions. A skilled digital researcher can easily examine many more cases, and online publishing increases the likelihood that more obscure sources of law will become accessible.

Technology and Client Value

Sophisticated clients expect their law firms to have modern office technology. It is hard to imagine these clients giving their business to a law firm that lacked facsimile and e-mail capability, Internet access, and the ability to deliver, receive, and handle digital documents. Staying current with the latest in law office technology costs money. Training staff to use the latest technology costs money. Compensating well-trained staff so they stay with the firm costs money. Adding and training new staff costs money. Computers, Internet access, Web pages, virtual private networks, and legal-specific software all cost money. Paying for necessary technology can be challenging if the lawyer only bills by the hour.

Unfortunately, the prevalence of technology within society affects client attitudes. One would have to have been a hermit over the last several years to have missed all the media coverage of the rise of the Internet, the dot-com boom and bust, Microsoft and its legal battles, and all of the many ways technology has affected our lives. Nearly all people believe they understand something about technology. People are familiar with the impact of computers and the Internet, whether or not they use these tools themselves.

Let's discuss how this applies to drafting fairly routine legal documents, by way of example. In an earlier age, one of the bundle of values that the lawyer provided to the client was the mechanical ability to produce documents. Not everyone owned or could use a typewriter. In the minds of both the lawyer and the client, this value was often overshadowed by the knowledge, education, and experience that the lawyer provided in producing legal documents. Many clients, particularly consumer clients, lacked both the knowledge and the means to prepare documents.

Now computers and printers are pervasive. Many consumers own them, and those who do not usually have access, either at a school or a library. Physically preparing and printing a document presents few challenges. There is no mystery. Many who have gone to get a bank loan, for example, have watched the bank employee quickly prepare and print the loan documents. Everyone understands that legal documents are rarely written "from scratch" but instead are compiled from forms and prior work product.

In fact, others may not appreciate how much time lawyers do spend drafting language for unique situations. Lawyers are trained to identify many potential pitfalls that must be avoided. They appreciate the evolving nature of the law and how court decisions and legislative enactments alter legal strategies and the language contained in the documents they prepare. They understand how adding a single unique aspect to a transaction may create the need for different provisions in several of the documents drafted. Those who do not regularly prepare such documents do not. Business clients in particular may use many forms generated on a computer for their office paperwork. While these may be generated quickly, they usually are essentially the same transaction being repeated with only the name, address, quantity, and price being changed. They see the paperwork only an a means to an end and, absent trouble, attach no value to the document itself.

As noted previously, sophisticated clients expect their law firms to have modern office technology. They may have reaped huge benefits themselves from technology upgrades, often directly related to their paperwork production and reduction. Consequently, lawyers are confronted more and more with clients and potential clients who believe that their legal matter is very routine and involves the lawyer "just filling out a form." Sometimes these clients seek to save money by completing the documents themselves. In other situations, they discount the value that the lawyer brings to a transaction and, mentally, the legal fees that should be charged for "just filling in a form."

In other words, the ease with which documents can be physically prepared has caused many to devalue the expertise, ability, and time that go into drafting legal documents.

These aspects of the technological revolution present a dilemma for lawyers. As we develop more effective methods of harnessing technology for speedy document preparation and document assembly, charging an hourly rate for the final steps that generate the document unfairly overlooks the investment the firm has made in designing its systems and effectively using its tools. But a switch to charging a fixed fee per document can generate a reaction if the client believes that this is merely an increase in the fees the lawyer is charging just to fill out a form.

This stresses the need for good communication between the lawyer and the client about the varied complexities of a legal matter and the value of the lawyer's advice. If the client believes that all he or she has received is a document prepared by using a computer to fill in the blanks, the lawyer's service will be seen as negligible and minimal.

Technology and the Billing and Collection Process

Effective use of technology in the actual billing process, however, can be a true "win-win" situation. Since most aspects of the billing and collection process are administrative in nature and not billable to the client or otherwise recoverable, creating efficiencies here has no negative impact on a lawyer's billings. A better billing process is a positive improvement for the lawyer in all ways.

Within a law office, the process of billing clients consists of the following general work processes:

- The lawyer records the time, the description of the work performed, and the charges whether time-based or task-based.
- The lawyer's secretary or accounting staff then integrates the other expenses charged and payments received within the prebill or ledger of the firm's records.
- The lawyer and firm then prepare a statement for the client reflecting those charges and previous payments received and retainers applied.

♦ The statement is then transmitted to the client in some manner.

♦ The lawyer (hopefully) receives from the client either payment or a request for clarification of the statement or additional information.

♦ If the statement is not promptly paid, the lawyer then institutes collection efforts for the amount due.

The discipline required on the part of the lawyer for the first step—keeping concurrent and accurate time—is, of course, more of a struggle for some individuals than others. Anecdotal evidence suggests that many law firms, particularly those in the solo and small firm category, have difficulty with instituting a process for the final step of the billing process: collection.

Let us briefly discuss how appropriate technology can be used to facilitate or improve each of the above steps in the billing process.

Recording the Charges, Whether Time-Based or Task-Based

What recording process is used for getting the records of fee charges from the lawyer's desk to the client's hands? In the traditional, or paper-based, system, the process is something like this:

♦ The lawyer writes the time charges contemporaneously on a billing sheet or diary.

♦ The billing sheet or diary is later delivered to or retrieved by the secretary or billing department.

♦ The secretary or a billing clerk types the information into a computer, hopefully being able to accurately decipher the lawyer's handwriting.

♦ After all billing, payments, and other expense charges are entered, the result is printed out in lengthy drafts or prebills.

♦ The prebills are then sent to the lawyer for review. The lawyer will hopefully not delay the editing and review by being distracted by other priorities.

♦ Any corrections or additions are rerouted back through the above steps until the bill is finalized.

♦ Then, after final approval, the bill is printed in final version and mailed to the client.

Contrast the above steps and potential delays with a more modern model:

♦ The lawyer enters time charges contemporaneously into the billing program on his or her own computer.

♦ The billing clerk enters payments and expenses into the billing program as they are received or incurred. The billing clerk or secretary can proof the time entries of the lawyer on a regular basis before creating a final proof.

- When it is time to finalize bills, the responsible lawyer is notified by e-mail to proof the final bills over the network. Each bill can quickly be proofed online without printing. Few changes are needed, since the attorney made most of the entries originally and the entries have been proofed by his or her secretary or billing clerk. Note that even though electronic proofing is possible, some lawyers and some law firms may prefer that the proofing be on paper for record-keeping and accountability purposes. Some people proofread much more effectively on paper than on a computer monitor.
- The bills are printed in final version and mailed or electronically transmitted to the client, often accompanied by a credit card payment option.

Clearly, the single greatest improvement in efficiency in the billing process would be to persuade lawyers to personally enter their time charges, whether for time or task billing, into the computer system. Many lawyers try to deny and resist this truism. Lawyers have, after all, been filling out time sheets by hand for a long time now. Some lawyers have poor keyboarding skills. But even a "two-fingered typist" can enter a brief billing notation in a process more efficient than the cycle of the lawyer handwriting information, then a third party interpreting the handwriting and entering the data, and then the lawyer or administrator proofreading the data. Voice recognition technology has evolved to the point where lawyers can simply dictate their time directly into the billing software.

There are different ways for the lawyer to enter the data. In a solo practitioner's office, the billing software may actually reside on the lawyer's computer, where time is entered directly into the billing software. With several lawyers and a networked office system, the method involves the lawyers accessing the billing software over the network or entering the data through simple "pop-up" windows.

Another method, which is growing in popularity, is to use another separate software application to record the data and export or link it to the billing software. Many lawyers and law firms use case management software to manage and track many types of information about their client files, including billing records. By entering the charges into the case management software, there is an advantage, with the lawyers having to be trained in only one primary piece of law office software. Another advantage is that the lawyers have the billing records within the case management system for quick referral, such as a client asking about the particular charge for a certain task or refreshing one's memory about the date of an event when the notes are unavailable.

Many software products are available in the case management software arena. This method of easily recording billable time or billable tasks is highly recommended due to the many other benefits to the law practice of incorporating the use of case management software.

Whether the lawyer enters data directly into the billing program or indirectly through case management software, this process clearly changes the way the lawyer interacts with the office billing system. Once the billing data becomes digital, it is more valuable. It can be used for interim reports, productivity evaluations, and many other law office internal matters besides the actual billing to the client. Accurate and accessible electronic billing system allow lawyers to establish budgets and set fees for many alternative billing options. It is therefore critical that charges be entered into the system at the earliest and least error-prone stage: contemporaneously by the attorney doing the task. Various court, business, and ethical requirements for contemporaneous maintenance of billing records have long made this abundantly clear. Because systems that avoid handwriting interpretation and proofreading help ensure the integrity of the contemporaneous records, such systems will soon be universally accepted as the norm.

We could not leave a discussion of the lawyer entering billing descriptions without mentioning the ABA Law Practice Management Section book *How to Draft Bills Clients Rush to Pay,* 2nd edition, by J. Harris Morgan and Jay G Foonberg. Every lawyer should be trained and regularly reminded that whenever possible, these statements—which are often too short—should reflect the effort expended by the lawyer and the value to the client. Bills are, in fact, a critical client communication.

Integrating Other Expenses and Payments Within the Statement and Firm's Records

When the lawyer directly enters most of the fees into a computer system, the staff has more time to make sure the expenses and other accounting items are in correct form. But even here, the process can be expedited. Most firms already use some sort of accounting software package. The ultimate goal is to achieve the single entry of expense data, spread across the system as needed. Too many small law firms (and a few larger ones) engage in double, triple, and even quadruple entry of the same data about an expense that should be borne by the client.

The following example of a system at its worst shows how many times data could be entered using a single check for a court filing fee. A lawyer is unsure of the exact amount of a court filing fee and so takes a blank check along when going to the court clerk to file the document. The lawyer then handwrites the check at the court clerk's counter, hopefully obtaining a receipt.

Upon returning to the office, the amount of the check is entered into the checkbook register by hand. Later the checkbook entries are transferred to an accounting program. (This is already the third time someone has entered this data.) Finally, a separate data entry is made to the billing program so the expense can be charged to the client.

Whether this is a trust account or an office expense account, these steps could be consolidated into one step. If the amount of the check is known before the lawyer goes to court, it could be entered into the accounting software and used to print a more professional looking check for the filing fee. The accounting program would either serve as the billing program as well, or easily share information with the billing software and any other office application that requires the information. Preparation of the check could theoretically handle all the steps listed in the preceding paragraph. Moreover, law office applications that handle all the steps seamlessly are affordable, even for solo and small-firm practices.

Preparing a Statement for the Client

State-of-the-art software programs for billing allow great customization of billing statements. Law firms should take advantage of this by taking the time to design a bill format that promotes the firm's image and provides a positive brand. Although it is not always necessary to use exactly the same fonts and designs or logos that appear on the firm's stationery, it is often highly desirable. A bill statement format that complements and is compatible with the law firm's stationery, fax cover sheets, and business cards supports the law firm's efforts at branding. This tying together of a law firm's image is critically important as the legal business environment grows even more competitive.

Earlier practices of using an old printer with less-than-stellar output to produce bills should be totally unacceptable to the lawyer trying to create a positive and professional image. Bills and statements are an important client communication and should be treated with care. Many clients and client representatives read bills with more care and attention than copies of court pleadings and substantive documents prepared by the lawyer. There is no excuse for a bill format that looks cheap or generic, no matter the size of law firm.

Transmitting the Statement to the Client

This step requires little discussion, as the only real value-oriented variable here is the timeliness of the statement in relation to the end of the billing cycle, the completion of the case or project, and the client's internal needs. The lawyer should be aware of certain time frames that will encourage and expedite payment, such as consumer clients' pay periods or the times that business clients pay their monthly bills. (For example, if a business pays its monthly bills on a fixed day each month, you may want to arrange to get the bills there a week before that date to allow time for review and processing the payment.)

In the future, many more clients will request bills via e-mail. In response to such a request, the lawyer should ascertain the client's objective. Does the client want a true digital bill that can be used in-house for internal communications (for example, text that can be copied and moved into other documents or e-mails), or does the client simply want a scanned image of the bill? Is there a preferred format, like PDF? Does the client understand that careless forwarding of an "e-bill" might compromise confidentiality or reveal litigation strategy? Will the client pay electronically?

Receiving from the Client Either Payment or Requests for Clarification or Information

Improving the mechanical handling of receiving payments from clients was discussed in the section concerning the integration of expenses and payments; the goal is to minimize the data entry while ensuring that proper credits are made. (This part of the process has many concerns outside of the scope of this discussion, such as security against misappropriation.)

Clients who have questions or concerns about bills usually contact the lawyer in charge of their projects, typically by phone for significant complaints. In larger firms, other staff persons or departments may be designated to handle such questions or complaints. To encourage clients to contact those persons or departments, it may be wise to program a notation on the billing statements, just following the total. A sample notation might read, "If you have any questions about this bill, you may contact our billing department by phone at 123-4567."

Some may be concerned that this will encourage complaints. But many of these requests will just be for information, such as whether the bill is the final bill. For disputed bills, it is still best to air disagreements and concerns as early as possible. Otherwise the client may simply set the bill aside without paying it and another month of labor (and billing) may be done by the lawyer before a problem is recognized. Opportunities for clients to have feedback are critical in any service environment, but especially when alternative billing methods are being implemented.

Instituting Collection Efforts for Balances Not Timely Paid

Many small law firms do not have clear collection policies, and firms of all sizes often tend to ignore their policies with special cases and other exceptions to the rules. Also, some lawyers have a tendency to identify personally with their clients and their clients' causes. It then can become difficult to assume the somewhat contradictory roles of championing clients in court or negotiations, for example, while dunning them for payment of past-due fees.

A collection policy should be determined in advance; exceptions to the policy should be rare, with any such decisions made by committee or objective partners. Basic law office technology allows firms of all sizes to implement collection policies. Sound business judgment requires the adoption of one.

Essentially, many steps of a collection policy can be handled with a series of diaried dates and form letters. This is one situation in which using the firm's word processing system to produce a series of similar letters on specific dates becomes quite useful.

A sample policy might include the following steps (with all periods of time running from the date of initial billing):

- ◆ *20–25 days.* A staff person can be assigned to contact the client by telephone to make certain there are no problems with the bill and to ask when payment can be expected.
- ◆ *30 days.* When a second monthly bill is sent out with the previous balance unpaid, it is stamped "Past Due" in red ink.
- ◆ *40 days.* An internal e-mail notice is sent to the lawyer, explaining that payment has not been received. This allows the lawyer time to intervene if there has been a mistake or some alternate agreement made with the client.
- ◆ *45 days.* The first collection letter is sent to the client. This is written in the "friendly reminder" style.
- ◆ *55 days.* An internal e-mail notice is sent to the lawyer, explaining that the client is seriously delinquent and that steps must soon be taken to rectify the situation. It is suggested that the lawyer telephone the client to discuss the matter.
- ◆ *60 days.* Included with this month's billing statement is a letter noting that the account is seriously past due and the firm may need to reconsider its continued representation if arrangements are not made within the next five days.
- ◆ *66 days.* The management committee meets with the responsible lawyer to assess any practical or ethical obstacles to withdrawing from the representation. Depending on the situation, notices may be sent to the client explaining that work has ceased and, in litigation matters, that a motion to withdraw has been prepared and filed.

Every lawyer and law firm must tailor the above example to serve individual needs. Some lawyers may see these dates as providing too much delay, while others may believe they are too rigid. Many will feel that a more personal one-to-one approach is appropriate.

The benefit that technology brings to this process is the rapid and inexpensive system of diarying the dates and generating the form letters. Too many times a lawyer will procrastinate in contacting a client about such an unpleasant matter, even after promising the partners that it will be done. Sending a notice to the lawyer a few days in advance of the firm's collection effort can motivate the lawyer to handle the matter personally before it reaches the next stage. The large-firm lawyer, whether partner or associate, who is concerned that too many of these delinquent client situations will reflect poorly on the lawyer in periodic evaluations may take a more proactive stance with client payment issues. The solo or small-firm lawyer who notes an inordinate amount of collection efforts by staff may determine that there is some greater problem, such as the lawyer failing to place enough emphasis on timely payment during the initial engagement process, accepting inadequate retainers, or making poor decisions during client selection.

Technology in Fee-Setting and Budgets

Technology in the form of an electronically based billing system is useful not only for tracking time charges, billing, and collecting fees, but also for establishing budgets for projects similar to those already handled by the lawyer, and even determining what can be charged in alternative billing options. In Chapter Four, where we discuss the foundations to developing alternative billing methods, we outline how to go through a task-based analysis and emphasize the necessity of examining closed files (and accounting and billing records) to create minisystems and predict fees. It is through the use of technology already present within most billing systems that these processes can be implemented quickly.

Nearly all computer-based billing systems on the market today have category and coding options that allow a lawyer to track not only similar types of cases and transactions in a larger "macro" context, but also specific components or tasks within the case or project in a "micro" context. If each case or matter is coded with a category (such as Merger/Acquisition, Incorporation, or Divorce) and possibly a subcategory (such as Merger/Acquisition, Asset Sale; Incorporation, Oklahoma; or Divorce, Uncontested w/o Children), then it can be relatively quick and painless to sort prior activities and collections to determine the time and resources needed for the last five or ten or hundred of those projects. If the lawyer time for an Oklahoma business incorporation averaged 3.8 hours with an average billing of $684 in fees, then perhaps establishing a fixed fee for such work at $750 might make some sense—particularly if using technology to develop an incorporation system with a document assembly program meant that the lawyer could reduce his or her average time to 2 hours and increase their realization rate from $180 per hour to $375 per hour!

Many billing systems allow the lawyer to separate billing slips into specific tasks and even integrate them into task-based billing and case planning. The ability to identify the costs and time required for certain tasks that fall within a case or project enables the lawyer to develop estimates and budgets for large projects. These billing systems allow the lawyer to answer questions such as, "What did the last fifteen depositions cost in similar cases?" or, "What was the average time it took to prepare the last ten revocable trusts for clients in their estate plans?" Being able to segregate information in prior matters is crucial to budgeting for future business and establishing alternative billing methods that the clients will accept.

Many large corporations and insurance companies have long championed the use of task-based billing as a means of reducing outside-counsel fees, creating efficiency in the billing process, and limiting the huge differences in fees charged by different firms for essentially identical work in contracts, claims, and litigation throughout the country. A task force of The American Corporate Counsel Association developed Uniform Task-Based Management System (UTBMS) billing codes that a number of large corporations have adopted to use with their internal legal staffs and with outside counsel. (UTBMS codes can be found at **www.abanet.org/litigation/utbms/**.) When UTBMS codes are used, law firms and their clients can budget complex cases more accurately, coordinate tasks more efficiently, create acceptable and uniform formats, and resolve many potential billing disputes before they arise. Many large firms transmit invoices electronically, which are then integrated into the client's system to test against budgets and billing rules. The result should be an electronic payment that is quickly remitted.

Substantive Systems and Document Assembly

Perhaps the best use of technology in alternative billing is the implementation of document assembly programs and systems, which generate documents in a fraction of the time it takes lawyers to produce them. By developing a substantive system and using document assembly tools—with stand-alone systems (such as HotDocs™), practice-specific programs (such as Cowles Estate Practice System™), internal systems within word processing programs (such as WordPerfect™ or Word™), or tools built into practice management systems (such as TimeMatters™, Amicus™, or ProLaw™)—lawyers can cut the time it takes to develop initial drafts of documents and thus build a platform for charging clients for the documents provided rather than for the time it takes to prepare them.

If a client needs a will or a business incorporated, he or she likely does not care how long it takes you to prepare the documents; they want to know what the cost will be for the corporation or the plan documents. By developing a substantive system using document assembly as a tool, lawyers can use technology to provide better and faster services to the client and make more money than if they billed the work by the hour.

An organizational system applied to a substantive area of practice can be an effective tool in addition to enhancing the delivery of quality legal services. A substantive legal system is a documented system for handling transactions, procedures or work flow that has the effect of reducing waste, optimizing productivity, and contributing to greater efficiency in the delivery of legal services. A substantive system could still be a manual forms system, but in today's world, a computerized document assembly or expert system makes the most sense. A substantive system enables lawyers to provide top-quality legal services promptly, thoroughly, and consistently. In short, law firms that use substantive systems with document assembly can deliver quality legal services for fair value while reducing the lawyer time involved in transactions and giving the lawyers more time to do something else (like working, marketing, or relaxing).

Beyond their utility in freeing up lawyer time, substantive systems can be used in many areas of law practice to market legal services. There are many areas of substantive law practice which lend themselves to substantive systems being used as an effective marketing tool. An example is the Corporate Representation Service™, a system developed by one of the authors of this book, which is described in more detail as one of the case studies in the Appendix.

Other substantive systems with document assembly are commercially available. The Cowles Estate Practice System is but one example of programs and complete substantive systems used throughout the country by lawyers who want to change the billing systems in their estate planning practices from hourly based fees to fixed fees. Colleen A. Cowles's book, *The Effective Estate Planning Practice: Procedures and Strategies for a Client-Focused Business* (American Bar Association, 2001), describes a substantive estate planning system in detail.

Knowledge Management Tools

If document assembly programs and systems are the current technology for alternative billing methods, then knowledge management will be the tool of the future. The most valuable asset in a law firm is its intellectual capital— not only the knowledge and wisdom of the lawyers, but the work product of those lawyers and the ability to reuse and share that work product within the firm and with clients. Knowledge management is about sharing and reusing knowledge.

Automated substantive systems are a part of knowledge management; they allow lawyers to develop and share a system with templates and forms that are used to create final documents. Practice and case management systems networked in a law office can also form a part of knowledge management. These systems can provide functions as simple as ensuring that new addresses are inputted once and are instantly available to the entire office, and functions as complicated as placing shared transaction documents on an extranet with client access to secure electronic conference rooms. Knowledge management is about technology, but also a lot more. Knowledge management is as much about the culture of the law firm that shares knowledge as about the method and tools used to accomplish the task. For a good resource on the principles of knowledge management, see *Knowledge Management* (Carl Frappaolo, Capstone, 2nd Ed., 2006) or go online to one of the top-rated journals in the field. (See **www.kmworld.com** or **www.brint.com** for extensive resources and links).

Law offices implemented concepts of knowledge management and reuse of prior work product long before computers existed. Paper "brief banks" and internal form books not only increased efficiency, but also helped provide a superior work product. Technological advances escalate these ideas. Thousands of briefs in research banks can be effortlessly searched using technology. Using most document management software, an entire firm's electronic client files that could contain hundreds of thousands of documents can be searched for names, terms or specific words in a matter of seconds. Similar transactions can be replicated to start a new project for a client. Knowledge management provides the tools to the lawyer to look beyond the billable hour in determining a fair fee for services. If the culture of the firm is to share research, knowledge, ideas, data, and even anecdotal information, then technology can capture that knowledge and help the lawyer extract it when required for the next project, case, or client need.

Most firms are only beginning to plan for this application of technology. Some law firms now have a Director of Knowledge Management. Implementing knowledge management tools requires lawyers to invest time and change old habits. After all, the best search engines built into a document management system can retrieve documents and data only if the system is designed properly and the data are entered into the system in the first place.

Transaction Fees: Sharing the Costs (and Benefits) of Technology

As the use of legal technology tools has increased, so has the lawyer's ability to share the costs of those tools with the clients—particularly if the tools help reduce the fees that would otherwise be charged for the services provided. Lawyers are more frequently building the cost of specialized programs into the fees charged a client, when those programs significantly reduce the cost and time required for the client's project. Depending on the nature of the transaction, the program costs are sometimes part of a fixed-fee arrangement, or they might be a separate charge in addition to an hourly rate or other time charge.

One common tool for which there is normally a transaction charge is one of the electronic research systems (such as Westlaw™ or LEXIS/NEXIS™). A lawyer may incur a charge for specific research or have a flat monthly cost arrangement, and then bill the charge as a flat rate or include the charge in an electronic-research hourly rate that might be different from the standard rate determined by the agreement with the client. A common tool used in securities practices is a licensed document assembly system that generates blue sky forms and certain Securities and Exchange Commission filings, for which the law firm might charge a fixed fee per filing, to cover both the technology license and the paralegal/lawyer time expended in completing the documents.

Some lawyers may be concerned that exposing too much law office technology to clients could affect clients' perceptions of their lawyers' value. However, modern-day clients expect their lawyers to incorporate technological tools in their practices, in the same way that many of these clients have been forced to rethink their business processes in light of new technological capabilities.

Collaborative Technologies

Lawyers sharing information with one another and with clients can be critical for moving beyond hourly billing as the only measure of value provided by lawyers to their clients. Technology can be used to share information over the Internet through extranets accessible to clients, lawyers, and other members of a project or case team. Extranets can provide cost-effective and secure Internet-based storage centers that allow documents, e-mail, discussion group threads, and other information to be stored in a secure area that can be accessed by those needing to participate. Different areas of an extranet can have different levels of security and access. Law firms are already building extranets for their clients as part of the normal delivery of legal services. These firms are not only generating revenues from the use of such technology collaborations, but also cementing relationships with clients. The immediate access to all relevant information that these clients enjoy makes other law firms without such tools less attractive.

Law firms and individual practitioners are also using the Internet and document assembly technology combined with expert systems to work with clients in developing standard documents for routine transactions, for which fixed fees—rather than hourly billings—are frequently the norm. An Iowa firm has a Web site where individuals can enter information online for their own simple wills. Another firm has established a loan document system in which the lender and borrower provide the information electronically and the documents are generated, reviewed, finalized, and e-mailed for closing without a paper draft copy being printed—all for a fixed fee. An international financial printer has developed secure Web sites to which multiple law firms, issuers, and underwriters have access, and where they can create, post, and edit documents for the workgroup to use before electronically filing them with the Securities and Exchange Commission. For additional information on collaborative technologies, see *The Lawyer's Guide to Collaboration Tools and Technologies: Smart Ways to Work Together*, by Dennis Kennedy and Tom Mighell (ABA Law Practice Management Section, 2008).

Conclusion

This chapter provides some examples and ideas demonstrating how lawyers can use technology to increase efficiency in their billing processes and to think beyond the billable hour. Many applications of technology are discussed elsewhere in the book, and some that we touched upon only lightly (or even ignored) are used regularly by practitioners. Technology can be the great equalizer between large firms and solo/small firms—not only by enhancing the practice environment but also by fostering creative ways to provide value to clients and bill appropriately for that value.

Developing the Case Plan or Transaction Plan

6

The "case plan" or "transaction plan" is a systematic writ-ten outline of what must be done to accomplish the client's objectives in a particular case or transaction. The detail and complexity may vary, depending on the assignment. In some circumstances you will be able to foresee the scope of services and what is required, while more complex mat-ters may involve unknowns that will require you to revise your plan periodically. Use of an alternative billing sce-nario increases the need for such an outline in advance, so that both client and lawyer can have a mutual road map as the matter proceeds.

The principle that underlies the case plan or transaction plan is that at the outset of any representation, you should map out or plan what must be done to reach the client's objectives. "Case plan" suggests litigation and "transaction plan" suggests some-thing other than litigation, but that is the only distinction be-tween these labels.

Why Should I Bother with a Plan?

Whether you are a solo practitioner or practice in a firm, it is im-portant that you communicate with your client about some fun-damental items: What have you been hired to do for the client?

How much will it cost? When will it be completed? Although a business client in a complex transaction may insist upon a written plan, the solo practitioner's consumer clients often need it more—since they are usually inexperienced and unfamiliar with the legal process, have little or no basis upon which to evaluate the technical or procedural nuances of the legal problem, and generally are nervous when dealing with lawyers. Whether in your fee agreement, a checklist, or a written plan, you must define the client's problems and needs, communicate your competence in addressing those problems and needs, and agree on a fee arrangement.

Developing a plan is an early stage of communication between you and your client. It is a game plan that forces both you and your client to develop and agree upon what is to be achieved. It requires a commitment of resources and can suggest the appropriate billing method. Ultimately, it can be the standard for measuring the value received. The goal is to give the client some certainty about the cost (or at least the process), which allows the client to make an assessment of value.

The steps that occur in organized practice management should start before you agree to accept the representation. These preliminary steps include (1) analyzing your prospective client, the objectives sought, and the type of issue presented; (2) making a preliminary examination of the facts; and (3) verifying the legal principles and the availability of enough expertise and staffing to undertake the representation. Developing a case/transaction plan is a logical way to carry out these steps.

The plan you develop is much like a game plan developed by a coach in an athletic event or a battle plan developed by a military commander. The common thread is to devise an approach that defines the problem to be solved and the resources that will be available, recognizing that there may be many variables or unknowns that will require adjustment as the matter proceeds.

For some legal matters that are reasonably routine, the plan can become part of the office practice manual or minisystem, prepared in advance and communicated to the client through the legal representation agreement, standardized checklists, and correspondence. For example, for a nonjudicial deed-of-trust foreclosure, each step can be systematized. The client's objective is to complete the foreclosure, to postpone the foreclosure, to reinstate the obligation, or to cancel the proceedings. Once started, the process can proceed until one of those conclusions occurs. If the deed-of-trust foreclosure is contested, the steps to be taken differ from the nonjudicial process, but the course is determined. All this can be clearly outlined to the client in the legal representation agreement, a standardized checklist, or correspondence that is prepared and already in a system. Many would not consider this simple illustration to be a "plan," but it is.

Both computer-based and manual practice systems (such as incorporation systems for business lawyers or estate planning systems for lawyers working in estates and probate) can be developed internally or purchased from vendors who have developed proprietary systems to handle those types of transactions. Such systems lend themselves readily to establishing fixed fees, which provide value to the client and higher realization rates to the lawyer.

However, many representations are not so simple. Because the steps to be taken vary by practice setting, area of practice, type of matter, and client objectives, you should work with the client to develop a plan specific to the representation.

Elements of the Case/Transaction Plan

A typical plan, whether for litigation or transactional representations, should be in writing and should be the common product of lawyer and client. The fact that it should be a common product does not negate the lawyer's obligation to have forms and other document assembly tools in place to make drafting a plan operate very quickly. After all, the goal is for the client to have the plan in hand at the earliest possible stage. For smaller and routine matters, this means that the client should be given the case plan at the same meeting where the lawyer is retained. It may be a part of the engagement letter or a separate attachment or timetable delivered at the same time. All plans should include the following elements, although in simple or routine matters, these may be combined with other elements and/or may not require detailed analysis:

1. Definition of the client's problems (both legal and nonlegal).
2. Gathering of the facts.
3. Initial legal analysis.
4. Statement of client goals and expectations.
5. Prescription of steps necessary to succeed.
6. Anticipation of uncertainties, unknowns, and possible alternatives.
7. Definition of the scope of the work.
8. Determination of the resources required, including who will be working on the matter with the primary attorney.
9. Forecast of schedules for each part of the process.
10. Definition of the client's duties.
11. Definition of the lawyer's and possibly support staff's duties.
12. Determination of the range of dollar values or the importance of what is at stake:
    a. for the case/transaction.
    b. for the legal expense.
13. Evaluation of the risks:
    a. to the client.
    b. to the lawyer.

14. Agreement regarding how the risks will be shared.
15. Determination of the billing method to be used.
16. Procedure for modifying the plan, which must provide for contingencies, unknowns, factors beyond control, changed conditions, and the need for possible revision in the case/transaction planning to meet changing conditions.

Some of the issues to be resolved in the development of the case/transaction plan should be included in the legal representation agreement. In simple or routine consumer matters, perhaps all the elements could be in the fee agreement. However, the case/transaction plan as a planning method can be more specific and detailed, particularly in more complex matters. It may involve checklists so that as steps are completed, you can have a written record of where you are and what needs to be done.

For example, in a complex case, a detailed plan might include names and addresses of known possible witnesses—favorable and adverse—with a schedule for interviews and possible depositions. All discovery would be included, again with a method for summarizing the filing of the testimony when discovery is completed for each witness. Key documents would be cataloged and indexed with an appropriate filing system for required retrieval. As the case evolved, all this information would be gathered in preparation for the ultimate trial.

If you were asked to do estate planning, the transaction plan would involve the necessary asset information, the names of the legatees or beneficiaries, the client's objectives with respect to providing for family or other needs or minimizing specific taxes, and the types of documents and resources needed to fulfill the plan, such as pour-over wills, revocable trusts, irrevocable life insurance trusts, various types of powers of attorney, and the like.

Once you grasp the concept and recognize the value of the type of analysis required to develop a specific case/transaction plan, you can adapt the general principles and features for your use on any matter—simple or complex.

Preparing in Advance

Establishing a case/transaction plan actually begins when you finish the last similar case or transaction. How many of us do a thorough review and analysis of a case or transaction at its conclusion? Determine what we did right or did wrong? Choose what we can extract from the case for future use—briefs, forms, research, ideas? How can technology assist us in providing this same service and value at a lower cost? Nearly every other profession goes through this or a similar process at the conclusion of an engagement. A "post mortem" meeting or project review after each engagement provides information that is invaluable in making the next similar engagement better and more profitable. Spending as little as one hour doing this post mortem to refine a case plan for the particular transaction as a part of your case closing procedure should pay dividends in future similar matters.

One of a lawyer's greatest assets is his or her old files, which can and should be prospected and mined for information and ideas to aid in the next engagement. Billing records hold critical information on the time and cost required to provide services of a similar or identical nature, which helps in establishing fixed fees or estimating fees in a case/transaction plan.

Setting Client Goals and Expectations

Early in the process of developing the case/transaction plan, you should elicit from the client his or her goals and expectations in the matter. This may not be easy, as the client often has not formulated a goal or may have an objective that is not disclosed specifically to the lawyer. Defining objectives may be an ongoing process.

It also is critical to determine, as early as possible and based upon the then-known facts, whether the client's goals and expectations are reasonable and attainable. For example, a personal injury claimant may have in mind a recovery of $5 million in a case that appears at the outset to have a settlement value of $10,000. No matter how good a job you do, the client will be dissatisfied if your appraisal turns out to be the final result. The stronger your agreement with the client that his or her objectives are reasonable, the better your relationship will be.

It is difficult to measure the "value" you will provide to the client until you know the client's objectives. Take as an example four variations in a simple marriage dissolution representation:

1. The client wants an amicable dissolution that is fair to both spouses, done quietly without antagonism and with adequate provision for family support. *The objective is fairness*.
2. The client indicates that although the dissolution of the marriage is inevitable, the entry of any decree should be delayed as much as possible, at least until after a major business transaction has been closed. *The objective is delay*.
3. The client indicates an intent to remarry at the earliest possible date and states that no matter the cost in terms of property settlement, you should get the marriage dissolved as soon as possible. *The objective is speed*.

4. The client is angry and vindictive, wanting to strike back against the other spouse in any way possible to repay the wounding the client has suffered. *The objective is revenge*.

If the lawyer does not understand the client's motives and objectives, there may be a mismatch. If the lawyer's approach in handling the dissolution is counter to the client's objectives, the client will be dissatisfied with the value received no matter how technically good the representation might have been. There may also be combinations of these objectives in varying degrees of intensity. Often, helping a client to clarify the most important objective is an important part of the representation process.

If you think in terms of a real estate acquisition rather than litigation, you can develop the same types of scenarios to reflect different client objectives. To illustrate, the client may wish to negotiate to purchase a parcel of land (1) to buy at any price because the parcel is indispensable for a planned development, or (2) to buy for investment if the parcel can be acquired at a reasonably fair market value, or (3) to buy for speculation only if the parcel can be acquired at a bargain price. Negotiating techniques might vary depending on the client's true objectives.

Setting realistic client expectations about time frames is important as well. In marital dissolution, a series of events usually follow in regular order. These may include filing and service of the initial pleadings, a response by the defendant, a temporary order hearing, various discovery procedures, a pretrial conference, court-ordered mediation or settlement attempts, and, finally, the hearing on the merits. Since most domestic clients are negotiating unfamiliar waters, time lines are a useful part of case plans. Although lawyers always orally explaine these time frames to their clients, providing them with written documents that they can take home and periodically review gives clients greater value.

Determining Billing Methods

Satisfaction of client objectives is tied to the choice of billing methods; the ultimate fee to be charged must relate to both the client's perception of value and the cost of providing the services to the client. You will learn more about the matter as you and your client develop the plan, and as you do so, you can determine an appropriate billing method that is fair to both you and the client. As with any other undertaking, the more times you develop a plan, the more skilled and effective you become.

Implementing Value-Based Billing

7

Using value-based billing requires you to rethink the billing process. You must manage your entire practice to ensure that clients are receiving value for their money. Thus, the ideas in this chapter are intended to stimulate thinking on innovative approaches not only to billing, but also to the conduct of the practice of law.

In changing from one billing method to another, you must consider what the change is, the effects of the change, the reasons why the change will be resisted, and how to find ways to overcome that resistance.

The old way of thinking associated with the cost-based method for billing by the hour was that hours equal value and leverage equals profit. As costs go up, rates rise as a multiple of costs. A whole generation of lawyers and clients grew up with—and had become accustomed to—hourly or cost-based billing as the predominant method. There is comfort in doing what is familiar. Whenever change is contemplated, it is necessary to analyze whether current conditions are the same as the conditions that existed earlier. If problems are different, the solutions should be different.

The cost-based method essentially favored lawyers, without regard to the benefit or value produced for their clients. This led to dissatisfaction on the part of many clients. As described earlier, when the market for legal services was expanding, the hourly billing method was seldom challenged and even came to be accepted almost as the standard approach.

In contrast, value billing is an attempt to equate the amount of the charge to the client's perception of value, or to tailor the billing method to meet the client's preferences. Implementing this method is more than just *billing for value*: it is *managing for value*. Managing for value means doing only those things that will produce a benefit. It means that lawyers exist to serve clients, not clients for the benefit of lawyers.

Implementing a change to a core office function, particularly one involving money, will no doubt stimulate a response and discussion among lawyers and clients alike. This chapter discusses the actual implementation of the new system.

Value Billing and Profitability

No matter what billing method you use, your legitimate interest is to be compensated adequately. The premise of value billing is that clients who receive value are satisfied clients, and satisfied clients make for a profitable and successful law practice. Moving away from hourly billing does not mean lower profitability; in fact, if value is produced, there will be mutual benefit.

The "realization rate," when traditionally and more narrowly defined, means the extent to which collections of fees equal fee billings. In the broader context, "realization" can be defined as the extent to which you are fully paid for all services performed. This implies that you are doing the right things and that what you do provides a benefit to the client. Thus, profits are linked to planning, wise choices of steps taken, expertise, and managing for value to the client.

The rate of realization then depends on both external and internal factors. External factors include client satisfaction (the perceived quality of the work product, the perceived efficiency in the generation of the product), market characteristics, client characteristics, and the rates compared with competitors' rates for similarly valued legal services. Internal factors include efficiency in generating the product, the mix of the persons doing the work (delegation of work to associates or paralegals), the effective use of systems and technology, timely billing and collection, legal and industry specialties, management attention to quality and value, and provision of assured quality to the clients.

The objective of value billing is to optimize realization by matching the fee to the value of the services and to deliver services profitably, given the client's perception of value. Value billing therefore forces you to understand the economics of your practice and focus on ways you can maximize the net income per partner. Here are at least five ways:

1. Increase chargeable hours per charging person (utilization). That is, people can work harder, longer, and more productively.
2. Increase overall fee realization. Do this by eliminating unnecessary work that provides no benefit to clients.
3. Increase the book of business per lawyer. The "book of business" means the amount of desirable and profitable legal work per lawyer that results from doing good work, having satisfied clients, effectively marketing services, and otherwise adding to the volume of the type of work that produces value.
4. Reduce costs.
5. Increase operating leverage by:
   a. adding associates and paralegals.
   b. reducing the number of partners.
   c. leveraging technology.
   d. outsourcing to lower-cost providers.

These techniques apply regardless of the billing method used.

Strategies for Profitable Value Billing

How can value billing make your practice more profitable? This approach to managing your practice suggests several possible strategies.

Seek a Higher Dollar Realization

First, you can move in the direction of work with a higher dollar realization. Two ways of doing this are to prune the client base and prune the lawyer base. You can also use marketing techniques designed to attract the kind of work you are seeking. For example, the marketing effort might have these objectives:

- Promoting the firm's reputation.
- Promoting clients' loyalty to the firm.
- Establishing new loyalties and expanding upon the existing base.

Finally, you can seek work with a higher dollar realization through the selective hiring of lateral partners whose expertise or reputations will attract higher-quality work.

Raise the Value of Your Service

You can also enhance profitability by increasing the actual or perceived value of your services. To increase the actual value of services, you might use these approaches:

- Through research and development, stay ahead of the pack.
- Do more for the client; redesign your product to be more effective.

- Use innovative approaches to dispute resolution.
- Focus on industry niches.
- Increase the quality of your services.

Here are some ways to increase the perceived value of your services:

- Improve communications.
- Improve speed and responsiveness.
- Improve availability.
- Increase senior counsel involvement and visibility.

Improve Quality

Improve quality as a means of increasing "value." For example, as computers have evolved from mainframes to personal computers, the price of computing has come down despite an increase in the capabilities and performance of smaller, less costly personal computers. Similarly, when handheld, battery-operated calculators, cell phones, digital cameras, and personal digital assistants each first came on the market, they had limited capabilities and were relatively high in price. Now, consumers can purchase a single piece of equipment that will do all of these functions and more for a very competitive price. The manufacturers of personal computers and handheld items have enhanced the quality and capabilities of their products and provided better value in relation to cost, which has resulted in their widespread use. The same should apply to legal services.

Reduce the Cost per Unit of Service

By cutting the firm's cost of providing a unit of service, you can boost the amount of revenues going to the bottom line if you do not change the fees received for the units of service. The most obvious way to do this is to optimize productivity (output of legal product per lawyer per time period). There are numerous sources of enhanced productivity:

- Better-trained lawyers and staff.
- Utilization of paralegals, associates, and/or outsourced research and drafting to lower-cost providers.
- Forms and systems.
- Automated research tools.
- Expert systems (computer applications designed to assist in decision making).
- Practice management and quality controls.

Also consider implementing a two-tier practice structure to recognize that in most law practices, some legal business is routine (the "commodity work" described in Chapter Three) and other practice areas are "unique."

Most law firms tend to treat all matters as having the same value from the viewpoint of both lawyers and clients. Physical surroundings, skill of personnel, and even office locations and outsourcing to research groups domestically or internationally can be restructured to reflect the difference in expertise required for different types of work. Once these distinctions have been made, the firm can selectively recruit personnel based on demands of either "volume" business or "custom" business.

Use Technology

You can create value by using technology to automate and improve services. Your office can utilize substantive law expert systems, document assembly, case management, and budgeting software. Using technology to create value normally involves the following steps:

1. Decide what you want to accomplish.
2. Consider the impact of technology on existing methods.
3. Determine the cost-effectiveness of the technology.
4. Select what to automate.
5. Select and develop specific systems.
6. Determine pricing for services.
7. Explain the new techniques to clients.

Technology also gives you the means to outsource research and some drafting to a lawyer or firm on the other side of the world in the afternoon and have the results waiting on your computer when you get into the office the following morning—increasing the speed and potentially reducing the cost of the services to you and your client.

Being at the forefront in the evolving use of technology gives pioneering firms competitive advantages. The promise of technology for the legal profession is that it will give law firms the flexibility to pursue alternative billing methods by lowering the costs of producing legal documents and services. See Chapter Five for a more comprehensive discussion of technology.

The payoff for the effective use of technology is rapid and flexible adjustment of pricing policy to market conditions. Not insignificantly, with efficient use of technology, pricing no longer needs to be determined solely by the amount of billable time required to produce the service.

Position on the Value Curve

The principle of the value curve, introduced in Chapter Three, suggests that the curve itself probably will not change a great deal. Changes would probably be at either the high end or low end, depending on whether the proportion of unique services increases as the law evolves or whether more and more services are produced routinely or stop becoming the sole domain of the lawyer.

To the extent there is change, it would be primarily on an industrywide basis and influenced by outside forces. However, the dollar value at any point on the curve might change, depending on the number of lawyers competing or the amount of services performed by nonlawyers.

Although the value curve itself remains quite constant, a lawyer or law firm may be able to move up on the curve in total practice, or by practice area, by fitting into both the external and internal factors. This is called "positioning," which involves fitting into a slot in the curve by taking a selective approach to law practice. For example, if you do commodity work, you can reduce that type of work and develop expertise in work that is at the high end of the curve. The curve does not change, but your position on the curve will have changed:

> If you increase the "actual value" by turning out a better product, you will move up the curve.
>
> If your clients have an increased perception and appreciation of value, the ultimate test, the effect will be to move you up the curve.

Clients' Perception of Value

There are ways to increase clients' perception of value. Perceptions can change if you concentrate on, and improve, some or all of the following factors:

- Image.
- Lawyer-client communication.
- Timeliness of services.
- Availability.
- Dependability.
- Response time.
- Convenience to the client.
- Efficiency.
- Effectiveness.
- Stability.
- Accountability.
- Fairness.
- Education of clients so they understand the value of the services.
- Education of clients so they better understand the responsibility assumed by the lawyer.
- Conveyance of a caring attitude.
- Doing the right thing.

These factors permit differentiation, which involves distinguishing the services that you can perform from those performed by other lawyers. The differences may be actual or perceived, but either type of difference is reflected as value in the marketplace.

Guarantees

Another way to build client loyalty is to guarantee performance, a concept that is not prevalent in the service industries. In contrast, guarantees of manufactured products are common. Some are restricted in scope while others guarantee total satisfaction. For example, the manufacturers of Zippo™ lighters guarantee that they will repair or replace any Zippo lighter without charge. The customer merely sends the lighter to the company, and back comes a lighter in good working order. No questions are asked! In maintaining a high level of service, Nordstrom™ stores accept the return of merchandise for credit or refund, again with no questions asked. What kind of guarantee could a law firm give that would be meaningful and would develop client loyalty and be of value? Here are some realistic possibilities:

- *Any phone call received from a client before 4:00 P.M. will be returned the same day.* If the lawyer is unable to do so, someone else will return the call to explain why the lawyer cannot, set a time when the call will be returned, and ascertain the problem or the message or provide the necessary information.
- *Agreed-upon deadlines will be met.* If the deadline for performance cannot be met because of uncontrollable factors, the client will be advised to that effect before the original deadline.
- *Written work products will be free of typographical or spelling errors.*
- *A written status report will be supplied at specific intervals.*
- *All appointments will be kept promptly.* No clients will be kept waiting more than ten minutes beyond the scheduled appointment time.
- *There will be no charge for the initial conference with each new client.*
- *Copies of all documents and correspondence will be sent to the client.*
- *There will be no charge for phone calls to or from clients of less than ten minutes' duration per day.*
- *At the end of each matter, a client satisfaction survey will be sent to the client.*
- *For each client, there will be a backup person who is knowledgeable of the status of the matters being handled for that client.*

Many of these suggested guarantees would cure some of the common client complaints. Perhaps more important, a commitment to these guaranteed performance standards would set the internal law firm requirements for client service. As part of the program for guaranteed performance, the firm should specify some adequate monetary benefit to the client in case the guaranteed commitments are not met.

Change: How to Bring It About

As with any change, sometimes it is easier to start on a small scale (for example, with one or two partners in a small firm, in only one practice area, or in one department of a large firm). That way, not everyone need be involved, as some will resist change or be slow to change. Remember, the lawyer or firm must first be convinced that there are reasons to change the methods of billing.

Before you approach the client, you need to undertake some internal analysis. Review a few closed files to examine the fees charged, the number of hours characteristically spent by everyone who worked on those files, and the procedures followed. (See Chapter Four for a more thorough discussion of reviewing closed files and bills.) Think about how those closed files could have been handled more efficiently. Then ask some "what if" questions about those same closed files. Assume you were considering a change from hourly billing to a fixed fee per case. Compute what the results would have been with the closed files if you had handled those matters for a fixed fee. How would that billing method have affected you? How would it have affected the client? What volume of work would you have needed to reach profitability on an average case?

If after completing your analysis you conclude that a fixed fee could be charged on particular types of cases, think about which clients send you that type of work. Which clients are most likely to be willing to innovate, to try something different? Pick the client that appears to be the best candidate. You need not, and perhaps should not, adopt the change across the board. Have a test run under the best circumstances.

Once that decision has been made, you must educate the client about the proposed change and persuade the client to try it. An example of a successful approach occurred when a banking client and outside law firm agreed to test the alternative method. A number of cases were assigned for handling, with half on a contractual-fee basis and the other half on an hourly billing basis. After the cases were concluded, the outside firm and corporate counsel analyzed the results and negotiated a mutually acceptable ongoing representation agreement.

It is not always the law firm that wants to alter the billing method. Sometimes a client wants to change how the lawyer bills for service. For example, in-house counsel may be dissatisfied with hourly billing and want to innovate. Corporate counsel who have arranged alternative billing methods tend to use the procedure just described. It starts with reviewing how cases have been handled and charged by outside counsel. When corporate counsel can view volumes of cases that have been handled by more than one outside firm, they can establish patterns. Whether the impetus for change comes from the lawyer or the client, both parties must practice good communication and be willing to try something different.

Often the push toward innovation comes from below. Assistant in-house counsel may need to convince the general counsel to change, just as the lawyer may need to convince partners, departmental chairs, the managing partner, and the executive committee of the benefits of innovation.

Case Study: Could This Happen in Your Office?

The associate in a law firm, John Young, enters the office of the department chair, Sara Head.

"Hi, Sara. Do you have time now to discuss an idea that I've been developing for some time?"

"Sure, John, tell me what's on your mind."

"You know that we have been handling a lot of nonjudicial deed-of-trust foreclosures for three or four banking clients. Most of them have been assigned to me, and my legal assistant, Jackie, has worked closely with me. In fact, with the systems we've developed, it seems we can do most of the cases on a routine basis."

"Yes, John, I'm aware of what you've been doing in handling those foreclosures."

"Jackie and I have gone back and reviewed all the foreclosures that we had in the past year or so. We know how much time was spent on each and by whom. We know the billing rates and the total fees that were charged. We averaged the time spent and the fee charged on a per case basis. I can give you a summary of what we found."

"That's interesting, John, and I'd like to look it over more closely. What do you propose?"

"Well, I think we could handle cases of the type included in our study for a fixed fee per case. Here on this schedule is what I think we could include by way of services and what we could charge per case. If the foreclosure became contested or if a stay order was entered by some bankruptcy court, we could cover that in the fee agreement. I know we might earn less on a few cases, but if we had enough volume, that should average out, particularly if one or more of our banking clients would give us all their work instead of splitting it as they now do. At the fee I suggested, we would have a profit, especially if we can improve our methods for processing the work to eliminate any unnecessary steps. The clients would be paying us less per case than the average fee paid during the past year, so they should be happy."

"This sounds interesting. Assuming we go ahead, where would you start?"

"Sara, I get along well with Sam Workout at First Savings. I think it would be best if we approached him with this idea to get his reaction. Then we could try the new method for a batch of cases. If it works for First Savings, we could then go to Second Savings and make the same proposition. I think the fixed fee would be attractive to them, because they always seem to worry about the total fee when we bill on an hourly basis."

"I'll study your figures, John. Let's meet tomorrow morning at ten o'clock to discuss this further. At the moment, it seems like a great idea. See you in the morning."

This scenario could lead to a fixed-fee billing method, but, with variations, one of the other methods of billing could be proposed. Similarly, the cast of a junior lawyer proposing innovation to the chair of a department could be changed to a partner convincing another partner, a law firm convincing the chief operating officer of a corporate client, a law firm convincing in-house counsel, an assistant in-house counsel convincing the general counsel, or in-house counsel convincing outside counsel.

The process starts with a willingness to innovate, an analysis of existing practices, a thoughtful review of the method of delivering services, a systematized method of producing legal services, a review of closed files to ask "what if" questions, a client relationship that is characterized by good communication, and a willingness on the part of the lawyer and the client to try something different.

Arguments in Favor of Changing Billing Methods

General Arguments

Following are some general arguments supporting a change from hourly billing to another method.

Match of Billing Methods to Client Needs

Aside from total costs, clients are concerned about the predictability of legal costs and risk sharing. Anticipate what each client desires and try to match that need.

Increased Client Satisfaction

Clients expect to pay for legal services, but if they are dissatisfied with the billing methods, they may sooner or later be dissatisfied with the services provided. Displaying a willingness to change can itself result in more satisfied clients.

Increased Incentive for Efficiency and Effectiveness

The analysis process should heighten the firm's ability to work efficiently and effectively, that is, to do things right and to do the right things. This is because analysis forces a review of what and how things are done. Once the firm abandons billing on the hourly method, it will have less of a tendency to do unnecessary things or to procrastinate.

Fairness

The injection of the concept of value, together with the recognition of the importance of the client's perception of value, direct attention to finding and using a method that most fairly measures the value of the services provided.

Recognition of Economic Realities

With increased competition and the fungibility of many types of legal services, services that are in the commodity end of the value curve are price-sensitive. This creates an imperative for efficiency, value, and appropriate pricing.

Reduction of Pressure for Expansion

Pyramidal organizational structures and reliance on leveraging through numbers have forced law firms to expand. As general economic conditions become less favorable, the way law practice is conducted becomes more important. If firms can increase profits through improved use of technology and more efficient production, they will be under less pressure to grow constantly.

Leverage for Profit, Not for Numbers

With increased efficiency promoted by the use of methods other than cost-based billing, plus hoped-for increased client satisfaction, law firms can concentrate on the "mean-and-lean" approach to profitability. Unbridled growth may be a thing of the past.

Increased Predictability of Legal Expense

When the time spent is the only basis for charging fees, a client cannot know in advance the total expense that will be incurred. Many alternative billing methods provide for predictable fees, thus satisfying a basic client demand.

Opportunity for Risk Sharing

Several of the alternative billing methods involve some sharing of risks between lawyers and clients. Risk sharing can promote efficiency, motivate lawyers and staff to produce better results, and demonstrate confidence in clients' causes. Thus, sharing risks can be mutually beneficial.

Impediments to Change

Despite the benefits, there are some understandable impediments to changing billing methods. Following are the ones most frequently enunciated:

- *Inertia:* "We have been doing all right. Why change?"
- *Lack of understanding of the concepts:* "This value billing seems like a lot of theory. It may work for others, but I don't see how it will work for us because we have a different kind of law practice."
- *Fear of change:* "I know how things work with hourly billing, but I don't know what would happen if we changed." (It is better to dislike the known than to fear the unknown.)
- *Compensation systems based on billable hours:* "If we did away with billing on an hourly basis, how would we know how to compensate our lawyers? We have always relied heavily on billable hours recorded." (The answer is to forget about billable hours as the major criterion for compensation and talk about total fees produced and received. Count dollars in the bank account, not hours logged.)
- *Fear that if systems and technology are major methods of producing services, and project management becomes a major role of lawyers, this would not be "practicing law":* "I didn't go to law school to just be a mechanic."
- *Generational difference:* "For the past forty years we have been doing hourly billing. Now you new guys want to change what has worked in the past."
- *Threat to the personal security of individuals whose role would be changed:* "For years I have logged more billable hours than anyone else in the firm, and now you guys want to change the rules."
- *Threat to the relative political power of the partner who generates a lot of hours, or to those associates who work for that partner but achieve relatively low realization rates on billings:* "I've got a good thing going, so why change it?"
- *Courts' reliance on time records in awarding fees:* "The courts may not recognize other billing methods, at least not for many years." (This is a valid objection in light of the typical time lag between new methods of law practice and courts' adjustment to those methods. After minimum-fee schedules were abolished, it took the courts a long time to adjust to hourly billing and time records. Nevertheless, only a small percentage of fees are set by the courts.)

♦ *Concern that under the Model Rules of Professional Conduct, a legal fee must be "reasonable":* "Under some of the methods of billing, would this be a problem?"

♦ *Uncertainty about the time needed to handle a case:* "What if this is a worst-case scenario? I can't estimate the whole project. There is no way a lawyer can anticipate all that might occur."

Overcoming these (and other) impediments to changing billing methods is what this book is all about. Identify the roadblocks in your firm and use the information in this book to change your firm and your practice for the better.

Concerns of Corporate Counsel

Since the first book in this series, *Beyond the Billable Hour,* was published, quite a few corporate counsel—as major and sophisticated purchasers of legal services—have expressed doubts about changing from hourly billing. One doubt is about "value billing." Some equate value billing with "premium billing" and object to the notion of being charged at a higher level. Others interpret "value billing" as a judgment about value made by the lawyer after the matter is concluded. The objection on this basis is that clients do not want to be at the mercy of the lawyer in setting the amount of the fee when there are no preagreed standards for making a fee decision.

Corporate counsel have diverse views about the billing methods of outside counsel, but at the same time, they express some common notions. In their role as clients engaging outside counsel, corporate counsel have these major objectives: cost containment (in terms of total dollars), predictability of charges (allowing budgeting and analyzing of the risks and benefits of a given course of action), cost efficiency (knowing that only what is required is being done and that it is being done effectively and efficiently), and risk sharing.

Legal services are generally recognized as covering a wide range of matters, from the repetitive and routine on the one hand to the risky and complex and infinitely complicated on the other. In between are nonroutine litigation and complex transactional matters, where the variables and uncertainties are difficult to foresee because of factors that are not controllable at the outset. Once these distinctions are recognized, it is possible to fashion appropriate billing methods.

Sophisticated clients who support hourly billing appear to do so only partly because of inertia. Generally, proponents of continuing hourly billing believe they understand how the method works, what the costs of producing legal services are or should be, and that they as clients can control the outside costs by requiring budgeting and discount rates based on volume, restricting what is done, prescribing who will do the work, and, ultimately, having the leverage to force work to be done on their terms because the outside firms wish to receive further work assignments. In the past decade, the increased role of inside counsel in managing outside legal work, or retaining specific legal work for processing by inside counsel, has made monitoring and controlling outside legal costs more effective.

In litigation matters where there are unknowns, a common technique is to use task-based billing to compartmentalize or segment the handling of the matter and to require a fixed fee or cap for a specific phase of the litigation, such as pretrial discovery. Periodic reviews are made at progressive stages, with the law firm and the client agreeing on a course of action and a fee arrangement appropriate for the next phase.

Some clients agree to pay a bonus for certain results, along with using the basic hourly billing method. This arrangement is designed to provide an incentive for effort, results, or speedy resolution of the matter being handled.

Increasingly, in-house counsel give legal work to lawyers or firms with specialized expertise in the subject matter being assigned. There appears to be less tendency to give all outside legal work to a single firm.

Conclusion

When changing from a cost-based billing approach to a value-based system, you must adjust the price of certain services. Some clients may perceive that some fees based upon cost are overpriced. On the other hand, some fees based upon cost may be underpriced in that they provide value, in the perception of clients, that is greater than now charged. Value billing is not "premium billing" as some contend, but an attempt to equate the price to perceived value.

Evaluating Results of the Use of Alternative Billing Methods

8

Evaluating the results of your billing process is an ongoing task. Conducting this evaluation will tell you whether you are making progress in becoming a win-win lawyer or law firm.

Remember that before you adopt any alternative billing method, you should determine your cost of doing business, set a desired profit margin, and attempt to predict the consequences—monetary and otherwise—of a change in billing methods. For example, Chapter Seven described how counsel for a bank and its outside counsel ran a test before entering a final agreement. That test involved handling a number of cases, comparing hourly billing with billing on a fixed-fee basis. Then, by mutual agreement, corporate counsel and outside counsel fashioned a more permanent representation agreement.

Review of Closed Files

As part of the effective management of your practice, you should institute a process for continuing review of your billing methods. Closed files can provide a wealth of information if you will make the effort to review them. For example, you can compare cases that were handled under a new billing method with similar cases that were handled with the previous billing method.

Move in the direction of analyzing each file or transaction when you either close the file or complete the transaction. Use the results of this case-by-case analysis to fine tune your billing methods.

When you open a new file for a new client (or begin a new matter for an old client), you probably use a routine form and follow a standard procedure. It is equally important to have a regular routine for closing a file, which allows you to evaluate results and review how you handled the representation. A form for file closing and evaluation appears as Figure 8-1 on page 93.

If you have in your file the case plan or transaction plan that set forth the objectives you and your client agreed would be sought, compare them with the actual results and determine the extent to which those objectives were reached. That will tell you two things: the extent to which the client received benefits from your services, and your skill level in projecting reasonably attainable objectives.

As part of this end-of-matter review, ask yourself these questions:

- ◆ What value did my efforts bring to the client?
- ◆ Were the results reasonably close to our projections?
- ◆ How could I have done a better job?
- ◆ How could I have been more efficient?
- ◆ If I had it to do over, how would I have done things differently?

From a review of similar cases, you may discern common features and procedures that can be converted to minisystems or complete systems. Frequently, once a lawyer or firm performs a service, clients make more requests for the same service. What may have started as a one-of-a-kind matter develops into repetitive work that can be systematized.

A retrospective review should lead to improved efficiency. For example, as individuals within the firm become familiar with processing a given kind of work, you can delegate increasing amounts of the work to the least expensive unit of labor competent to perform that service. A review of closed files can also disclose forms and agreements that you can convert from customized agreements into generic forms or agreements. Failing that, the review will at least lead to the preservation and indexing of prior work products for future use.

Analyzing profitability is part of the review process, so some sort of cost accounting will be advantageous. Once you regularly assess the profitability of a specific type of work, you can move toward eliminating the unprofitable work and increasing the type of representations that will place you higher on the value curve.

Figure 8-1   Checklist for Closing a File

File name and number	
Responsible lawyer	
General description of the matter	
Was there a written representation agreement?	Yes No
Billing method used	
Did actual time/cost exceed opening estimate?	Yes No
Was there a case/transaction plan?	Yes No
To what extent did the actual results reach the initial stated objectives?	
What value did you bring to your client?	
How could you have done a better job for your client?	
What would you have done differently?	
Can any systems or minisystems be developed from this file?	Yes No
Identify any forms, pleadings, or memos for the forms file	
Are there forms that can be made into generic forms for the form file?	Yes No
Do you anticipate work of a similar nature in the future?	Yes No
Was this matter profitable to the firm?	Yes No
Have you discussed with the client whether the client was satisfied with the handling of this matter?	Yes No
Summarize the client interview	
Did you do any cross-selling with the client?	Yes No
If you had it to do over, would you use the same billing method?	Yes No
If no, what method would you use?	
What technology was used on this matter?	
Could this matter have been handled more profitably by some other individual or method?	Yes No

Additional comments:

I certify that I have personally completed this form on this _____ day of _____, 20____.

_____
Responsible lawyer

Client Audits

An important aspect of evaluating results of the use of alternative billing methods lies in determining the extent of client satisfaction with that prior work. How do you do that? As noted in earlier chapters, communication between the lawyer and the client is critical. Lawyer-client communication includes learning the client's degree of satisfaction and perception of value.

As part of the procedure for closing files, firms often use client audits, surveys, or questionnaires. These ask a client his or her feelings about the handling of the matter just completed. If there is a problem that needs correction, the audit may point the lawyer in the direction of rectifying the shortfall. A form questionnaire appears as Figure 8-2 on page 95.

If the client expresses satisfaction, the door is open for cross-selling additional legal services, which is yet another important reason for conducting a review. There should be a systematic procedure for following up on any cross-selling opportunities that are identified.

Performance Evaluation

Another benefit of the review process is the opportunity to evaluate the level of competence of the person or persons who performed the services. Performance evaluations can be tied to compensation decisions, and can provide the basis for expanded responsibilities in making future work assignments.

Profitability Analysis

Billing methods will vary from firm to firm, from department to department, and from individual lawyer to individual lawyer. The type of work may dictate a certain billing method. Some lawyers will be more innovative than others. Individual lawyers may experiment with alternative billing methods on one or two matters or cases before adopting them for all matters of the same type. A practice group may decide to experiment with some alternative billing method, even though the firm as a whole has not recognized the advantages of innovating.

Consequently, it may prove interesting to make some in-house comparisons of profitability based upon these differences. If two lawyers within a firm do the same type of legal work but use different billing methods (such as time rate by one and fixed fee by the other), you could compare their profitability. Determine whether the difference in profitability is due to different billing techniques.

Quality of Life and Quality of Work Product

Another component of the review process, although it may be difficult to quantify, is determining whether there is any apparent difference in the

Figure 8-2   Confidential Questionnaire

	Y	N	Comments
1. Are you treated by the attorneys and staff in a courteous and professional manner? If not, please elaborate.			
2. When the firm handled a legal matter for you, were you kept fully informed of all pertinent matters relating to that matter?			
3. Have the legal fees and other charges been clearly and adequately explained to you? If not, how can we better explain them?			
4. Are our fees reasonable in light of the nature of the services we have provided you?			
5. During the last 2 years, have you used other lawyers to represent you? In what areas? Have you been satified with their services? With their fees? If not, why?			
6. Have you referred others to our firm? Would you refer others to our firm? If not, why?			

7. Please make any comments you feel would assist us in better serving you in your legal needs:

_____

_____

_____

_____

_____

_____

8. Optional:

Name: _____

Address: _____

Telephone #: _____   Fax #: _____

E-mail: _____

lawyers' quality of life resulting from the use of a specific billing method. Criticism has been leveled at the hourly rate billing method because it places such high emphasis on recorded billable hours. Stress, pressures, and the resultant lack of job satisfaction are sometimes attributed to some firms' requirements for billable hours. The review process can provide a means of escaping the "hourly rate syndrome" if the lawyer or the law firm can see ways to allow people to work smarter rather than longer.

The review process can help lawyers evaluate work product quality. Lawyers and firms can look for differences in the levels of client satisfaction and work product quality that can be attributed to the billing method chosen, and can use what they learn to help correct poor-quality work. The review process can also target for reward those individuals whose work is consistently good.

Conclusion

Systematically evaluating results requires discipline, as does consistently using written representation agreements and developing case or transaction plans. However, the discipline required to institute these methods results in a win-win law practice.

Alternative Methods of Billing

Alternative methods of billing as they now exist fall into several general types. The key to selecting a billing method is to pair the client's needs and expectations with the method that will most equitably measure the value of the lawyer's services.

Fixed or Flat Fee

The fixed or flat fee is the price that will be charged for defined services. It may be the total fee for the engagement or may apply to segments of the total services. It may stand alone or be combined with either an hourly fee or a contingent fee. An example might be a fixed fee for incorporating a business or preparing a will or a trust agreement.

Contingent Fee

The contingent fee is a charge that depends on results achieved. It requires clear agreement as to what the desired results will be as well as what is not covered by the fee. Those results may be positive (direct) in the sense of achieving a desired objective or negative (reverse) in the sense of avoiding exposure to liability. A contingent fee may be combined with a fixed or flat fee, or with hourly billing. A common example would be a fee charged in a personal injury case based upon the recovery. An example of mixing a contingent fee with a fixed fee might be a fixed fee for preparing a securities offering with a contingent or "success" fee if the offering closes and is funded.

Hourly Rate

Since the late 1960's, hourly billing (sometimes referred to as time-rate billing) has predominated. It is predicated on the keeping of accurate, contemporaneous records of time expended by lawyers, legal assistants, and other staff members. The hourly rate for each fee charger is intended to cover the cost of production plus a profit factor. Therefore, knowing the cost of production is important (although many lawyers do not have reliable cost data to determine what their costs are to deliver legal services). To some extent, hourly rates are market-driven, particularly at the commodity level, and can reflect lawyer expertise and anticipated value at the high end of the value curve.

Hourly billing has developed some non-time-related aspects such as minimum time charged for particular services—for example, minimum time entries of one-quarter hour or minimum entries for each letter or phone call. These should be (but often are not) clearly explained to clients in the fee agreement.

Many lawyers or firms have different rates for different fee chargers and different rates for a specific lawyer depending on the type of service, the client, the subject matter, or other variables. These variations recognize that the value to the client will differ and that time spent per se does not accurately measure the fee to be charged.

This method can be combined with contingent fees or fixed or flat fee billing.

Blended Hourly Rate

The blended hourly rate is a hybrid of the hourly rate. Instead of specific hourly rates for individual fee chargers, one rate applies to all hours billed on a matter. This fee arrangement is found more often being used by larger law firms in large cases or transactions where the client has negotiated the fee.

Fixed or Flat Fee Plus Hourly Rate

In this hybrid method, the portions of the services that can be defined as to scope of services are charged on a fixed or flat fee basis, and the portions of the services that are not capable of being defined because of variables or uncertainties are charged on a time-rate or hourly basis. It can be used in both litigation and transactional matters. Numerous variations can occur, and the sequence of the method of charging may vary.

To illustrate the use in a transactional matter, in an estate planning assignment during the initial phase when the objectives of the client are being determined, asset information is being gathered, and tax ramifications are being determined, the method can be hourly. When the plan has been determined and what will be required can be defined, the preparation of documents and services necessary to complete the assignment can be charged on a fixed or flat fee basis.

To illustrate the use in litigation, a flat fee can be charged for handling what appears to be routine litigation, with some agreement as to what services are included for that fee. If it is necessary to do extra work, there can be an hourly charge for services beyond the original defined scope.

Hourly Rate Plus a Contingency

By combining hourly billing and a contingency factor, the client and the lawyer are sharing risks within the limitations of the representation agreement. Since a portion of the fee will be hourly, the lawyer is guaranteed a minimum amount. This is true whether the hourly fee is based on regular hourly rates or the agreed upon hourly rates are lower than the regular rates. That will guarantee the lawyer some payment but leave the client some risk.

As in straight contingency agreements, the client and the lawyer are both motivated to obtain the maximum results, since both will benefit.

It is important to define clearly the way that the contingent fee will be measured. If the achieved result justifying the contingent fee is not directly expressed in dollars, the agreement must spell out the amount of the contingent fee and how it will be measured. For example, the basis for the contingent fee might be obtaining a rezoning, acquiring a business, or obtaining a restraining order, all of which need to be assigned a value or tied to the fee amount that will be paid.

Percentage Fee

Typically, percentage fees have been based on a schedule of fees related to the amount involved in the matter being handled. The amount may be predetermined or may, in some instances, be related to the amount ultimately determined. Examples include a percentage of the value of estates being probated, the amount of a real estate transaction, and the amount of a bond issue. The percentage rate may be constant or graduated.

Task Based Fee

A hybrid of a fixed fee arrangement where the fee is based on identified tasks or components of the transaction such as the total square feet being developed, the loan amount or tasks or phases of a litigation matter. The measuring method is usually predetermined based upon the task or anticipated development or transaction but may, in some instances, be adjusted based upon changes encountered during the representation. The task-based method can also be used in budgeting complex matters even when the billing method is based all or in part upon hourly rates and time spent on particular tasks. Many larger businesses are requiring task based budgeting in litigation matters with approval required before billings can exceed the budget for the defined task.

Retrospective Fee Based on Value

The retrospective fee based on value differs in approach from most of the alternative billing methods in that the exact amount of the fee is not known to either lawyer or client until the matter is concluded. However, the representation agreement can set forth the factors that are to be considered in setting the final fee. Often these are the factors set forth in the Model Rules of Professional Conduct. It is possible to provide either a maximum or minimum fee that will be charged. The amount may be combined with an hourly fee in setting a minimum. The amount of the fee should be determined by the lawyer, not the client—although some firms using this method give clients a suggested fee which can be changed by the client or a range from which a client can set the fee.

Unit Fee

The unit fee is a subspecies of the fixed or flat fee in that the lawyer charges a fixed amount for a specific service, irrespective of the actual time spent in providing that service. For example, a lawyer could have fixed charges for each letter, phone call, and deposition. This approach normally is combined with hourly billing for services not included in the unit billing. Some representation agreements provide that, for a specified service, the lawyer will charge either the unit fee or the hourly rate fee, whichever is greater.

Relative-Value Method

The relative-value method combines elements of hourly, fixed or flat fee, and value billing. The relative-value method of billing involves creating schedules that break down the lawyer's services by subject matter and by task and assign a "relative value" or multiplier to each. Each fee charger can be assigned a different basic rate or charge, which is then factored into the equation. There are variations in this method as used by individual practitioners who have developed their own schedules. Proprietary systems also exist.

Inherent in this approach is a determination or judgment in the first instance of the value of each component service or task. This assumes that tasks performed by a lawyer differ in value, whereas straight hourly billing assumes that all time spent in performing various tasks has equal value.

Once the relative-value schedules have been established, the base rate factor can be changed, thereby changing the fee.

Lodestar Method

The lodestar method of setting fees had its origin in the federal court system in *Lindy Brothers Builders, Inc. v. American Radiator & Standard Sanitary Corp.,* 487 F.2d 161 (3d Cir. 1973), and has been adopted in some states. In an attempt to have an objective system that could be applied by the courts with some consistency, the method involves multiplying the hours spent by a reasonable billing rate per hour to determine the "lodestar." Then that amount is multiplied by a factor, such as 1.4, 1.7, 3.0, or 0.8, to recognize factors other than time spent.

Court decisions have restricted the factors that may be considered as a multiplier, contending that those factors are "subsumed" in the hourly billing rate. For example, "expertise" originally was a factor in determining the amount of the multiplier but now is generally considered to be reflected by the hourly billing rate. Uncertainty of payment remains a factor for the multiplier.

Courts often set billing rates that are below the market and sometimes will disallow a portion of the hours expended if the court deems the hours unnecessarily spent.

One objection to the lodestar method is that using it to approve fees takes up too much court time.

Statutory or Other Scheduled Fee System

The amount to be paid for legal services is spelled out in some statutory enactments, in schedules for prepaid legal service plans, or by purchasers of legal services on a volume basis. Some fees are imposed, some are negotiated. Some fees may be fixed or flat; some systems prescribe methodology. Some schedules are in fee-shifting situations; some reflect government imposed social policies.

Retainer—Availability Only

The availability-only retainer, sometimes referred to as a "pure retainer" or "right-to-call retainer," is characterized by payment to the lawyer of a fee for which no direct services (or limited services as specified) will be performed. In exchange for that fee, the lawyer makes a commitment to be available when requested and to refrain from representing either parties adverse to the client or competitors of the client within a specified time period.

This method is not widely used. It normally is used with a lawyer who has high-level expertise or prestige.

The funds, when received, belong to the lawyer and should not be deposited into the client's trust account. The majority rule in jurisdictions that have considered the issue recognizes the distinction between "advance fee deposits," which are client funds and must be put into a trust account, and "retainers," which are funds paid by a client to secure a lawyer's availability over a given period of time. The funds are considered earned at the time of payment and need *not* be put into the client trust account.

Retainer As a Deposit Against Future Services

The retainer as a deposit against future services differs from the payment of an "annual retainer."

The retainer as a deposit against future services is not per se a billing method, but actually a credit policy technique to ensure that the client will pay for services to be rendered or for disbursements to be made on behalf of the client. When the lawyer receive these funds, the lawyer must place them into a client's trust account and may withdraw them only after performing services or making disbursements in behalf of the client. At the conclusion of the representation, the lawyer must return any balance to the client.

Some such agreements require the clients to keep the funds on deposit at a certain level and replenish them when they drop below a certain level. This is done to even out cash flow for the lawyer and to ensure that funds will be available to pay the final bill.

This arrangement can be used with a variety of billing methods, as it is a deposit against future charges, however computed.

Case Studies and Fee Letters

To illustrate the practical application of some of the concepts discussed in this book, this Appendix contains case studies and reproduces some actual fee and representation agreements from firms of all sizes around the country. All illustrations are real-life approaches to the problem of billing fairly.

Case 1: Fixed Fee Corporate Representation
Case 2: Alternative Billing in Estate Planning
Case 3: Fixed Annual Fee for Small Businesses
Case 4: Virtual Law Office
Case 5: Fixed Fee Loan Documents Makeover
Case 6: Flat Fee Transactional Practice
Case 7: Moving to Value Pricing

Exhibit 1: Letter Giving Alternative Fee Options to Client
Exhibit 2: Formal Fee Agreement (Hourly or Contingent)
Exhibit 3: Increased Hourly Rate for Negotiations; Contingent Fee if Litigation Is Required
Exhibit 4: Alternative Billing Proposal for Either Hourly Rates or Reduced Hourly Rates with a Contingency Fee if the Business Is Acquired
Exhibit 5: Agreement for Fixed Fee Representation of a Bank for Major Collection Litigation with Bonus Clause
Exhibit 6: Fixed Fee Corporation Representation Service Election Form
Exhibit 7: Fixed Fee Retainer Agreement for Handling Insurance Defense Cases Based on a Prescribed Volume of Cases
Exhibit 8: Fee Agreement Incorporating Hourly, Fixed, and Unit Fees for a Real Estate Development Project

Alternative Billing Case Studies

Fixed Fee Corporate Representation

Name:	Robertson & Williams
Location:	Oklahoma City, Oklahoma
Size of Firm:	Nine attorneys
Practice Area:	Corporate, securities, estate planning, oil and gas, and general civil trial practice

Mark A. Robertson, co-author of this book, has used alternative billing methods for years in his corporate and securities practice. "Our firm has an extensive corporate practice in which we represent many small and medium-sized businesses. Our services include advice on structuring businesses, incorporation documentation, contract and employment work, mergers, acquisitions, real estate matters, dissolutions and other general corporate work. We utilize a number of substantive systems for doing this legal work and bill a lot of it on a fixed fee or combination fixed and success fee basis."

One such system the firm has used for a number of years is the *Corporate Representation Service*,™ which prepares annual meeting minutes (or a memorandum of action in lieu of a meeting), acts as a service agent, performs a corporate compliance check, and prepares special meeting minutes for clients for a fixed fee of $150 per year. (See the election form listed as Exhibit 6 in the Appendix.)

The firm has a computer-based system in place that generates correspondence, reminders, minutes or memoranda, and questionnaires, which in most instances requires 10 to 15 minutes of a lawyer's time per corporation per year. Some corporations may require several hours of a lawyer's time, but the average, spread out over several hundred corporations, still makes the work quite profitable for the law firm—and yet a bargain for the clients. Robertson said that in 2007, the realization rate was over $900 per lawyer hour!

Once yearly—usually in late January or early February—the firm sends out an election form, a questionnaire, and a bill for $150 to its corporate clients. The completed questionnaire enables the lawyer to determine what should be included in the annual meeting minutes and whether any special meeting minutes need to be prepared. "Most of the corporations we represent have bylaws that require an annual meeting in the first three months of the year, so 90 percent of the work is completed by the beginning of April," says Robertson. If the annual meeting will be held at a later date, the date is docketed in the firm's docket system and the minutes or memorandum of action are prepared when the meeting takes place.

The firm created a simple database to store the information for each business participating in the service, which includes basic corporate information such as the corporate name and address, officers and directors names, meeting dates, and the like. The information is updated with receipt of updates from the client along with the questionnaire. The data is then merged with forms in the firm's word processing software to develop everything from draft meeting minutes or memoranda, correspondence, reminders, as well as the election, questionnaire, and the bill.

"An additional benefit of the system we developed is that payment is usually made at the time the client sends in the election and questionnaire so there are very few collection issues," says Robertson.

The firm uses this pricing strategy with its *Corporate Representation Service*™ to attract new clients in addition to generating significant additional work as a result of the audit questionnaires, which often uncover additional legal needs of the client. As service agent for the client, the law firm's litigation practice can also benefit. By using this substantive system to do corporate work, the firm can organize its corporate work better while marketing additional services.

Robertson also reported that the same *Corporate Representation Service*™ database is used in forming corporations and limited liability companies, which are also billed on a fixed-fee basis. "Our incorporation documentation in our word processing system has the same merge codes as our CRS documents so once the information is entered in the database, we don't have to re-key it when the client elects to use our annual service," he said.

Many of the firm's small business clients want to know what something is going to cost before they go forward. If they can be told that forming a corporation or a limited liability will cost $1,000, which includes the documents, filing fees, book, seal, stock certificates, and initial tax qualification filings, they are more comfortable and likely to engage the firm for the work. The firm can use its systems to increase the realization rate for the work performed. The use of these types of substantive systems in the corporate, estate planning, and even in the securities area have boosted the firm's realization rates in these areas and given the clients what they have long asked for—a certainty on the amount of legal fees.

Alternative Billing in Estate Planning

Location:	Los Angeles, California
Size of Firm:	Solo Practitioner
Practice Area:	Estate planning

A recently retired lawyer in Los Angeles shared her thoughts on hourly billing alternatives and value billing. "My sense is that the term value billing is intended to reflect a method of billing centered on capturing the full value to the client of services rendered by a law firm and communicating to the client that value. My experience tells me that effective billing must be bilateral. It must reflect the perspective of the producer, i.e., the attorney, and the perspective of the consumer, i.e., the client. One measurement of effective billing is billing that reflects what the attorney perceives is a fair fee, given the services rendered; results in full payment of the bill within a short period of its receipt; and leaves the client satisfied with the services rendered and with the professionalism of the attorney."

She had developed and successfully used in her estate planning practice for many years a two-step method of billing—namely, "hourly" fee and "documentation" fee. The hourly rate is used for services rendered in order to arrive at a blueprint, i.e., a plan, which will be used to draft the necessary document. The hourly rate also is used for major document modifications requested by the client after the initial draft of the document has been prepared by the lawyer, in accordance with the blueprint. The documentation fee is a flat fee that is charged for producing the individualized (i.e., customized) framework document, which is based on the blueprint.

The documentation fee is a composite of variables, such as complexity of document, uniqueness of document, tax-sensitive nature of document, tax benefit of document, expertise required, priority timing required, risk aspect of document, client attitude, and desire to perform a particular service at a particular time. The documentation fee is not established until the plan framework is worked out in detail. The services for developing the plan are billed on an hourly basis.

The lawyer successfully used this two-step billing method in her estate planning practice. The billing method was explained to new clients, in writing, prior to their first appointment. Once the blueprint is arrived at, the estimated fees (both hourly and documentation fees) were discussed with the client prior to the end of the initial meeting and the client is asked to sign a fee agreement and to pay one-half of the documentation fee in advance. By this action, the client is reflecting a commitment to the plan from the beginning. The retainer amount is placed in the lawyer's trust account until a draft of the documents is sent to the client, at which time the amount is withdrawn and placed in her business account. The balance of the documentation fee and the hourly fees charged is due at the time of the signing of the estate-planning documents. This fact is reflected in the fee agreement and is confirmed in the cover letter that is sent to the client with the draft documents. Out-of-pocket costs for items such as photocopying are billed at the time of closing as well. If there are costs that are required to be advanced after the signing such as recording costs, postage, etc., those costs are billed when they are incurred—usually with in a few days of the signing of the estate planning documents.

The lawyer reported that the results of this system have been positive in a number of respects. If a potential client did not feel that her proposed fee for preparing a document was fair, they never get past the initial meeting. If the documents were prepared, the client was highly motivated to complete the project because a significant investment already has been made, i.e., one-half of the documentation fee already has been paid. Because the balance of the payment is due on signing of the documents, her receivables were minimal. She also pointed out that this bifurcated system of billing could be used in any area of practice involving framework documents such as incorporations, deeds, leases, buy-sells, and employment agreements.

Fixed Annual Fee for Small Businesses

Name:	William Gaines "Billy" Ellyson
Location:	Richmond, Virginia
Size of Firm:	1 lawyer, 1 full-time staff
Practice Area:	Counseling very small businesses
Web site:	http://www.ellysonlaw.com

William Gaines "Billy" Ellyson is a true believer in the benefits of utilizing alternative billing methods. Ellyson believes that he has established many more positive client relationships by charging his clients an annual fee rather than a fee for each legal matter or each hour spent working.

Throughout his career, Ellyson felt there was something wrong with traditional law practice, at least for him. He tried it in a traditional law firm environment. He tried it while also managing a law firm. Then he tried it as a solo practitioner. He realized the traditional business model of a law firm that matched legal services with charges based on time actually conflicted with his view of good client service.

Ellyson decided to transform his practice by representing only one type of client—the entrepreneur setting up or operating "a very small business." He reasoned that he could handle the requirements of small businesses on a fixed-fee basis because they were generally predictable.

So, Ellyson instituted his fee for these entrepreneurs: $500 per year plus an initial set up fee of $45. For this annual fee, clients may call on Ellyson for general legal advice along with the preparation of many standard documents, such as employment agreements, leases, buy-sell agreements, and business entity formation papers.

"In my experience, the distance between lawyer and client increases in direct proportion to the uncertainty the client feels about legal fees. The aim of the annual retainer is to make certain that there is a safe environment in which to conduct a business relationship," Ellyson writes on his web site, http://www.ellysonlaw.com.

Certainly there appears to be a ready market for this type of arrangement since so many new small business startups operate on a shoestring budget. But capping the majority of matters at only $500 per year seems a bit intimidating to most lawyers. (Ellyson has a few exceptions to the rule. He charges $1,000 for the purchase of a business and negotiating with the Internal Revenue Service. He makes it clear that he refers out certain types of matters such as litigation and real estate closings).

Once he decided to abandon the billable hour and the prospect of large fees from a single client or matter, some changes in practice setting were mandated. Ellyson had to greatly reduce the overhead, reduce paralegal staff, and move to a more affordable office location. Technology had to be more effectively utilized and the processes for document preparation were standardized. ProLaw® is used as the primary office software package for client information storage and document assembly.

While $500 might sound like a small legal fee to many lawyers, Ellyson says that it is a lot of money for many of his clients. They do not expect cut-rate services in return. But these clients are also happy with getting the answer by phone rather than expecting a legal memorandum. This is especially true because a lot of the advice Ellyson provides is motivation and common sense business advice rather than legal scholarship.

He notes that many individuals who work as independent contractors can benefit greatly by forming a business entity and paying attention to the tax ramifications of certain items.

Another aspect of Ellyson's philosophy is to frequently give away free advice. He often gives speeches to groups of individuals contemplating an entrepreneurial adventure. He strives to deliver practical advice and discusses pricing, business organization, and saving money on taxes.

Ellyson believes that other lawyers would benefit by giving away more of their advice. Being more open and available to the public, especially those with an interest in your area of expertise, has to be beneficial. He has set up a network of other professionals who are willing to dispense some free advice to his clients.

He holds free brown bag lunches for his clients every month with guest speakers. He accepts as many invitations to speak to civic groups as he can.

Asked whether he had any concerns of too many clients wanting services at the same time, he says, "the law of averages will save you on that." If he does have a flood of work that comes in at the same time, that situation is no different than in most law offices. Some more time spent working by the lawyer and a bit of patience from the clients will help you through those periods.

Another of the great rewards of this practice model is assisting those who otherwise might have proceeded without legal advice and gotten into trouble. Hopefully, they appreciate being steered through dangerous waters and become loyal long-term clients.

As a lawyer who will not profit from potential litigation, he feels that he has credibility when he advises his clients about the impact of litigation.

Ellyson freely admits that this practice style is individually suited to him and is not for everyone. Spending your days coaching and mentoring small business as they strive for success can be very rewarding, but also heartbreaking on occasion. Sharing the challenges of entrepreneurship is a source of great motivation for Ellyson. No doubt some clients have grown or will grow into companies with more complicated needs than Ellyson can serve. But all of his clients know how to show their appreciation for a job well done. When the statement comes in the mail for $500 for the next year's attorney's fees, they can pay it.

Virtual Law Office

Name: Kimbro Legal Services, LLC
Location: Wilmington, NC
Size of Firm: Stephanie L. Kimbro, solo practitioner
Practice Area: Estate planning, small business law, family law
Website: www.kimbrolaw.com
Blog: www.kimbrolaw.blogspot.com

Stephanie L. Kimbro believes in using the latest in available technology to handle billing, establishment of the attorney-client relationship and payment.

"I use technology to negotiate the payment process," says Kimbro. "My law office runs on Virtual Law Office Technology (VLOTech), which is a secure Web application. The alternative billing method that I use is part of a patent pending technology, a part of which is referred to as a dual escrow release system."

Essentially her clients register online through her virtual law office and create their own homepages. They then request the legal service that they would like to have her complete. The VLOTech Web application then places the request on her case queue so she can provide the client with a price quote.

"Sometimes I have to ask them more questions to clarify what they need done," she says. "But in most cases I have an idea of what I will be charging for those services. I establish the scope of the legal work to be done by explaining specifically what will be covered in this fee."

117

"In many cases, I already have this language written out and will just tailor it for the client. Then I reply with the standard response for that type of legal case. This could be compared with a standard retainer agreement in a traditional law office. I set the price this way and the VLOTech application sends a note to the client's homepage that they need to accept the price quote and terms of the scope of representation to proceed."

"The client then has to accept the price quote by reading through the terms of representation and clicking on the 'accept price quote' button before I will begin working with them. Once I have completed the legal service, I notify the client and if the project is the drafting of a legal document, then I upload the document(s) and mark them as final products. The VLOTech application will only allow the client to download their document or view my work for them after they have paid for my services."

The client is notified that the work is done. The client has two options: they either pay online, in which case their legal document/work is released simultaneously to them, or they may pay by personal check. There is then a delay until the check has cleared before "releasing" the final product to them online.

"This dual escrow release system protects both the client and me," says Kimbro. "It lets the client know the upfront cost of their legal services and keep track of the status of the work. At any time they may ask me questions through their homepage. It protects me because once the legal work is done, the client cannot take the final product and then refuse to pay. Clients also appreciate the convenience of paying online with a credit card. I have run my practice for over two years with the VLOTech application and have not yet had to deal with collecting from a client."

While there are some matters than are handled by Kimbro with other types of billing arrangements, the majority of work is handled with the online dual escrow release system.

Kimbro believes that this system allows her to serve more clients.

"Practicing online with this system has allowed my solo practice to double its business each year," she says. "The Web application expands my client base to the entire state where I practice law. I work in a small town in North Carolina and have clients in Charlotte and Raleigh several hours away. Clients are comfortable with this fixed-fee billing method and purchasing fixed-fee legal services online. On the personal side, the flexibility of this form of practicing law has enabled me to stay at home with my young child while also continuing to run a growing solo practice. I work on the weekends, evenings, mornings, and during my daughter's nap times. I am able to get in a full work week using this system."

The fixed-fee system has received almost universally positive feedback from her clients.

"The comment I hear the most often from clients is 'it's about time,' " she says. "I get the sense that the general lay public does not trust the legal system or attorneys. Many of my clients act grateful when I tell them what they can expect to pay, especially my clients who are middle-income individuals who have families. They need the ability to budget legal services and the billable hour does not allow them to do this safely. Again, many of them have told me they don't trust attorneys to bill them honestly, which is a shame. I think that is a misperception of our profession that I hope those of us using alternative billing methods will be able to dispel."

"Many clients, if they have dealt with attorneys in the past, do not understand how fixed fees work. The key to this type of alternative billing method is clarifying the scope of the legal services to be performed and making sure that the client understands that if it is necessary to go beyond that scope then I will have to charge them an additional fee for those additional services or refer them to another attorney. So far, this has not been a problem because of the dual escrow release system that requires the client to accept those terms before proceeding."

"My clients bank, pay bills and invest online so why wouldn't they want to purchase legal services through a secure Web application as well? Practicing with a virtual law office allows me the ability to be personal with my clients and build personal relationships but in a way that allows both of us to be flexible and work our lives and financial needs around the legal case, rather than the other way around."

Kimbro invites others to visit her site and review the process she uses.

"Please feel free to check out my virtual law office at www.kimbrolaw.com or register for a homepage to see how my clients interact with me. My vlo operates on the proof of concept version of VLOTech but the company (www.vlotech.com) is moving a larger group of attorneys online with the newest version of the Web application soon."

Fixed Fee Loan Documents Makeover

Name:	Ambrose Law Group
Location:	Portland, OR (branch office in Bend, OR)
Size of Firm:	Five full-time lawyers, plus one of-counsel lawyer and eight nonlawyer staff
Practice Area:	Real Estate and Business Consulting
Website:	http://www.ambroselaw.com/

Several years ago the Ambrose Law Group was moving gradually to alternative billing. Then a "law firm makeover" offer from *Fortune* magazine stepped up the pace of progress, which turned out to be a great benefit for the firm. This professional makeover included alternative billing staff realignment and use of improved technology.

The Ambrose Law Group had a successful boutique real estate finance practice. The matters that it handled were mostly transactions. They handled some litigation, but only for existing business clients.

They had been approached by clients who wanted them to handle the real estate closings, as well as preparing the documents for the transactions at a fee known in advance. The clients wanted a competitive price even though they were not actually paying the fees. (The buyers pay out of closing proceeds). In this way the clients could make certain that the total cost of their transactions was competitive and predictable. So the firm did research on the many prior closings that they had handled over the years and was able to identify the variables and calculate a method of predicting fees in advance.

But this project also got them thinking more about value and what value they truly brought to the process. Janis K. Alexander, Chief Operations Officer for the firm noted, "With real estate closings you are not just paying for the loan documents themselves. You are also paying for the insurance premiums that the documents have been done correctly. Our research made clear that there was a lot of predictability of costs with these matters." With the new price structure in place there was one immediate result; they started doing more loan closings.

But then they agreed to accept *Fortune* magazine's offer of covering them through a law firm makeover. The makeover team included Ron Baker, co-founder of VeraSage Institute and well-known billing reform evangelist. The makeover included technology improvements, as well as changes in billing practices.

The changes were not easy. But soon benefits became apparent, including the ability to expand the legal services that they were providing.

"Soon we moved into entity formation," said Alexander. "There might be several limited partnerships or other entities that needed to be created to accomplish a transaction and there was no reason we shouldn't provide those services to our clients. So we started creating all of the entities for developments going on in real estate. Even now we are continuing to revamp as things continue to change. Limited liability companies are more frequently used and then we are called upon to draft the operating agreements and possibly be involved in other aspects of their formation."

Alexander said that the main lesson they learned from Baker was that pricing is the key.

"He said never let people price who just can't handle it," she noted. "Some people can do great work but are really poor at pricing. They may do great legal work, but they don't think highly enough of themselves to be good at pricing."

Even today the firm has several "pricers" and several lawyers who do not handle pricing. That is probably just fine with them. Meanwhile those in the firm who have developed expertise in pricing continue to hone their skills.

"Now we never take a piece of new work unless we have quoted (and agreed upon) a fee," says Alexander. This requires a great time commitment in advance of taking on a matter. But she says it is better to invest the time in advance than have to do collection of unpaid bills.

Another key to pricing is providing for variables. Just as a construction project might have various "change orders," a legal project may also have "change orders" as either circumstances of client's needs evolve.

The benefits for this firm have been astounding.

With the technology improvements, Alexander estimates that they complete ten loan packages in the time it would take for four previously.

Clients have started mentioning the firm's technology and fee structure to other potential clients.

Within the first two years, gross revenues for the firm were up 75 percent and net income was up 160 percent.

There is an excitement among the lawyers doing their jobs in a more positive way. Recruiting and retaining good legal talent is easy because lawyers want to practice in this type of environment. Everyone feels more productive.

Founding partner David Ambrose is pleased with all of the changes that have taken place in his firm. The *Fortune* magazine article called him a revolutionary. But he would probably rather be known as a lawyer who provides great service to his clients.

Flat Fee Transactional Practice

Name:	Law Offices of Jeffrey C. Neu
Location:	Red Bank, NJ
Size of Firm:	1 lawyer, 2 staff
Practice Area:	Internet and technology companies and transactions
Website:	www.jeffreyneu.com

Jeffrey Neu has adopted a flat fee approach. Generally, this means that the client is quoted a flat fee in advance for a transaction or other matter. He believes that this approach is attractive to the business client for reasons of clarity and budgeting. He also uses this practice as a marketing tool.

His Web site states:

> "Flat Rate billing is not just lawyer friendly, it is business friendly."

> "Our firm does not count the minutes we are on the phone. With flat-rate billing, you will never receive a bill for an email or listening to a voice mail. Our lawyers do not rush off the phone so that two minutes equals six, or that an email costs you $50. We quote you a project or regular representation cost, and stick to our promises."

With the adoption of this type of flat-fee billing approach, the determination of the fee is of critical importance. Neu determines this fee by considering a number of factors. Most of these are objective, but some smack of art as much as science.

An initial consideration is personal interest in the project. "If it is something I don't want to do, or am not interested in, the base 'get me involved' figure may be higher," says Neu. "If it is a company and product that I really enjoy working with, the figure may be lower."

The next consideration is the overall value of the transaction. Generally speaking, if the transaction has a higher value, then the total fee goes up according to a sliding scale, starting at 10 percent of the value of the transaction with the percentage decreasing as the transaction value increases. A smaller transaction, in the $30,000 range for example, might well generate attorney's fees significantly less than those that would be charged on an hourly basis. "But at some point it just isn't worth it to get an attorney involved [on an hourly basis], so I make the call if we want to get involved and then whether that is of value to the client," Neu explained.

After the two primary variables are considered, Neu weighs four additional factors:

1. The representation of any party with an opposing interest.

The lack of an attorney on the other side of a matter can reduce fees, as can an attorney with whom the firm has had favorable experiences in terms of reasonableness or efficiency. On the other hand, a known attorney with a propensity to drag out matters or be unreasonable can negatively impact the fees.

2. The complexity of a matter.

Every lawyer can appreciate that the more complex or unique a project, the more expensive it is. Complexity can have a significant impact, as it can make a higher valued project drop considerably, or a lower valued project costs go up considerably.

3. Specific requirements or provisions from the client.

"Special demands from the client on specific provisions are significant. If there are things that are going to require a solid argument and serious approach and strategy towards, then I as an attorney provide more value," says Neu. It is not just that specific needs are more time-consuming, but that if there are complex negotiations or complex arguments or scenarios to be researched and prepared, the experienced attorney brings additional value to the process.

Here increased fees are sometimes attached to the success of attaining specific results for the client in a negotiation.

4. Timing.

If there is a rush, then a premium is charged, which is often true under hourly billing situations as well. If a client wants it done next week, then it costs more than if they want it done in three weeks.

According to Neu, these billing methods have been enthusiastically embraced by both lawyer and clients.

Neu is a firm believer in the positive impact this has had on his practice. How has this impacted your practice and your life?

"I love it. The best part is, although I still track my hours that I work on deals for personal efficiency side of things, I feel more valued, in better control, and have a more honest and straightforward communication with my clients. Time is a little crazier at times because I still have to meet deadlines, manage projects, and be on top of my calendar, but I often feel that there is a higher return on my time. Efficiency, skill, and that 'je ne sais quois' are rewarded, as opposed to just punching time. It takes into value more than a billable hour, and values according to what you can accomplish for your client," he says.

What feedback have you received from clients?

"My clients love it from multiple aspects. The first is that they can talk to me as much as they want about a project. The second is that on occasion if the bill is going to be quite large, we set up a payment plan right from the get-go. Several of my clients are in the under $10 million revenues per year range, and a six-figure legal bill for one month is difficult to manage. So we may spread the bill out over two or three months. They are happy that they can budget, although I have to front a bit of the load, I am happy to not have to harass for payment. Lastly, they look at it from a practical standpoint of looking at their legal needs and what they want to do, and assessing it with what they can afford to do. It fits legal practices into a budget and part of doing business rather than a guess," he states.

Of course, there were learning hurdles and missteps as experience was gained along the way.

"In the beginning I priced projects quite low, and that was a bit annoying, as my hourly return went down considerably when I undershot," said Neu. "That also can generate the negative feeling like being taken for granted. But as I have slowly learned and tracked the amount of time required for a project of different values, I can better assess not only the amount of time it takes, but also the kind of value I provide with my client using me versus another attorney on a project."

"It is also important to assess the client more than anything else in a flat-fee billing situation. Taking things into consideration such as whether they have worked with an attorney before. If they have not, sometimes it is better to do the first project on an hourly basis, so they understand the time and effort being put into a project. If they have worked with attorneys before, it is usually very easy to work with them, and they will automatically see the value," according to Neu.

Moving to Value Pricing

Name:	Peterson & Waggoner, LLP
Location:	Rochester, Indiana
Size of Firm:	3 lawyers, 4 staff
Practice Area:	Probate, commercial & business law, real estate and estate planning
Website:	www.peterson-waggoner.com

We thought it would be useful to visit with one law firm that had moved to value pricing fairly recently. Ted A. Waggoner, managing partner of Peterson & Waggoner, LLP, agreed to discuss with us the early stages of the transition. As he notes, there are some negative or at least challenging aspects that go along with the positive changes.

The first question has to be "So how is the transition to value pricing going so far?"

"I have been satisfied with the process, where once we established an agreed attorney's fee, I don't have to continually review to determine 'is the client paid?'" said Waggoner. "I also have more comfort that by doing an agreed value pricing fee, that we are in agreement on the scope of the work to be done, and the client has more control over the case."

What has proven to be the greatest challenge?

"It has made establishing client relationships more difficult, due to the need to invest time engaging in more discussion and conversation with the client. Several have not hired us, since we are still learning the communication needed. But others have been pleased," he stated. He believes that the communication aspects of the process are a critical element.

At this point, he says that he does not have enough detailed feedback to fully assess client acceptance and reaction. But he is encouraged enough to continue down this path.

Have there been any problems or "lessons learned" that you wish to pass along to others?

"When I act tentative, the client gets uneasy about billing. This happened previously, but then I would try to minimize the bill. Now we communicate our concerns through the 'yes—likely—maybe—who knows?' structure, and we get better understanding," he indicates.

The type of approach that stresses the contingencies and their likelihood of occurrence is a sound one. One needs to have some written documentation following the discussion.

Do you have any further comments or information you wish to provide?

"The books on value pricing are important, especially *Pricing on Purpose* by Ron Baker. I saw the value of the book in the thorough explanation of the various theories behind the actions. The theories start with lessons from Economics 101, and move forward through our responsibility to the legal profession," said Waggoner.

Exhibit

1

Letter Giving Alternative Fee Options to Client

The fee letter in Exhibit 1 provides the client with three fee options. The letter covers a proposed engagement to assist in preparing a private placement memorandum for the client to sell interests in a limited liability company. After an analysis of similar work, the law firm was able to present clients with different alternatives on how they wanted the fees to be charged—a fixed fee with a contingent success payment, a reduced hourly rate with a premium payment at closing, and a regular hourly rate arrangement based upon the time it takes to handle the matter. It has been the author's experience that in most instances, clients prefer a fixed fee that can be budgeted—even in matters as complex as securities offerings. Over the last 20 years, more than 90 percent of our private placement fees have been on a fixed fee with contingent payment, with an average realization rate of over 150 percent of our securities hourly rate.

[Date]

[Name Prefix] [First Name] [Last Name] [Name Suffix] [Title]
[Organization]
[Address 1]
[Address 2]
[City], [State/Province] [Postal Code]

Re: <u>Legal Representation and Fee Agreement</u>

Dear [Salutation]:

It is a pleasure having the opportunity to represent [organization] as corporate/securities counsel for the proposed private placement for the _____ project. We are pleased to undertake this representation. The remainder of this letter will outline the scope of the current private placement project and representation and the legal fee proposal for your consideration.

Scope of Representation.

The scope of the work required for a private placement by your Company (using a Regulation D offering) is to prepare the Private Placement Memorandum (together with the exhibits) for use in selling the member interests in the limited liability company. We will also need to file exemption notices or requests with appropriate state regulatory authorities.

In addition to the foregoing, the law firm will assist in preparing any state and federal reports, forms and other filings for selling. We will also assist in preparing the appropriate escrow agreement and other documentation for use in the offering at whatever bank you select to act as escrow agent.

Fee Proposal

I think that it is both appropriate and helpful to a client for me to outline in writing this firm's legal fee structure and, when possible, estimate the legal fees or give a fixed quote for the required representation. I believe it to be good business practice to discuss the subject of fees with a client at the beginning of our representation.

The fees charged for legal services traditionally are based upon a combination of the following factors: (a) the complexity of the matter and the degree of expertise required to handle the project; (b) the amount of time involved; and (c) sometimes the results obtained on the client's behalf. The nature of the project will often determine how the fees are charged. The fee arrangement should be established at the beginning of the representation and should be clearly outlined in writing or thoroughly discussed with the client so there are no misunderstandings. I prefer to use a fee letter that both the client and the law firm agree to.

The present scope of the legal work required is outlined under <u>Scope of Representation</u> above. I am confident that our law firm can handle the work required in a timely manner and for a fee that is fair to the Company. The fees for securities work done by most qualified law firms are charged at a premium over standard rates due to the specialized skills and high risks involved. I have found most clients in today's economy have requested a fixed fee quote for securities work as an alternative to an hourly rate, since it is easier to budget. I would like to suggest the following **alternative** fee arrangements, which incorporate these requests and have worked for several clients in the last few years:

Fixed Fee with Contingent Payment

- Payment of a fixed non-refundable fee of $10,000 payable as follows: $5,000 upon the acceptance of this fee arrangement and $5,000 upon the Private Placement Memorandum being completed and delivered to you. This would be for the securities, tax, blue sky in [_____] and [_____], and the other work outlined above for the offering under <u>Scope of Representation</u>.
- If the offering is successful and sufficient subscriptions are received to do an initial closing, an additional fee of $8,000 would be due at that closing.
- Any additional state filing work (outside of [_____] and [_____]) would be on an hourly rate basis at a reduced rate of $250 per hour (securities rate is $300 per hour) plus any filing fees, costs, etc. We will need to identify those states you wish to sell in before we can estimate the fees and expenses.

Reduced Hourly Rate with Premium Payment on Closing

- We would do the securities, tax, blue sky, and other work outlined above for the offering under <u>Scope of Representation</u> at a reduced hourly rate of $250 per hour (our securities rate is $300 per hour). Instead of requiring a retainer, billing will be done every other Friday, delivered electronically, and paid by the following Tuesday.
- If the offering is successful and sufficient subscriptions are received to do an initial closing, we would charge **an additional** $100 per hour for the work already performed. All work following the closing would be charged at our securities hourly rates at the time (currently $300 per hour).

Regular Hourly Rate

- We would do the securities, tax, blue sky, and other work outlined above for the offering under <u>Scope of Representation</u> at our securities hourly rate of $300 per hour. Instead of requiring a retainer, billing will be done every other Friday, delivered electronically, and paid by the following Tuesday.

Other Required Payments and Fees

- All major expense items such as filing and registration fees, travel, and printing expenses will be paid directly by the Company. Expenses advanced by the firm such as long distance, copies, fax, etc., using our published rates will be billed monthly and are due on receipt.

I believe the fee quote is quite reasonable for a private placement; our normal hourly estimate for a private placement of a partnership or limited liability offering runs $15,000 to $22,000 (due to the tax issues that need to be addressed) and can run over $25,000 if problems arise or there are a large number of states in which the offering is being sold.

Billing Procedures. We keep detailed records of the expenses we incur and, where appropriate, the time we spend on a project, and bill the work regularly to keep the client informed of our activities on his behalf. Each statement is carefully reviewed to determine whether a charge is justified before it is sent. Unless otherwise requested, the statements will contain a brief summary of the nature of the work and the costs advanced. In addition to the fees, you will be billed for all costs and expenses advanced on your behalf including filing fees, court costs, photocopies, facsimile charges, long distance, travel, and other out-of-pocket expenses. A schedule of our current charges is available on request. Any large or extraordinary expenses will be billed to you directly by the provider and are due on receipt. Our policy is to provide the client with a current summary of what was done on a particular matter. We encourage clients to ask questions and discuss our services and fees when the statement is received.

Summary

After you have had an opportunity to review this, please give me a call and we can discuss which option you prefer.

Very truly yours,

For the Firm

Exhibit

2

Formal Fee Agreement (Hourly or Contingent)

The following Exhibit 2 is a formal fee agreement that has optional provisions that can be used to cover both an hourly billing arrangement and a contingency fee arrangement. The form also includes a guaranty of payment.

Legal Representation Agreement

Effective Date: , 20   [City], [State]

This Agreement is made between [Name of Client(s)] ["Client(s)"], [Address of Client(s)]; and [Law Firm], [Address], [City], [State] 73116 ["the Law Firm"].

Statement and Subject of Employment

Client(s) retain(s) the Law Firm to represent Client(s) as counsel for Client(s) in a matter involving [name(s) of defendant(s)] and potentially other parties, based upon investigation, regarding [describe general nature of case] ("the Matter"). ("The Responsible Attorney") will be the attorney in the Law Firm who will have primary responsibility for handling the Matter, although other attorneys in the Law Firm may participate in the Matter. The Matter may actually compose more than one file [e.g., if separate claims are made on behalf of Client(s) against Defendant or other persons or entities whether or not the other persons or entities are parties to this case; or if separate claims are made by Plaintiff against Client(s)]. Regardless of the number of files the Law Firm opens for the Matter, all files related to the same subject matter are considered one transaction and constitute one Matter.

Client(s) authorize(s) the Law Firm to investigate the facts and research the law pertaining to the Matter, including potential claims and/or defenses, to determine the factual, legal, and economic viability of the Matter. Client(s) further authorize(s) the Law Firm to effect a resolution of the Matter and to settle or institute such legal action, including preparing documents, filing a claim against Plaintiff or another person or entity not a party to the suit, answering the petition or counterclaim, conducting discovery, and presenting the Matter for trial, as may be advisable in the Responsible Attorney's judgment.

Client(s) authorize(s) Law Firm to employ personnel inside and outside the Law Firm to perform necessary services to facilitate Client('s s') Matter. Representation of Client(s) by the Law Firm in the Matter will not commence until Client(s) and the Responsible Attorney have signed this agreement and any retainer payable at the outset of this representation is in fact paid by Client(s).

Representation of Client(s) by the Law Firm in an appeal related to the Matter is not included in this agreement. The Law Firm's representation of Client(s) in any appeal related to the Matter, if agreed upon between the Law Firm and Client(s), must be included by a written addendum or in a separate written fee agreement signed by Client(s) and the Responsible Attorney. Although the Law Firm may agree to represent Client(s) in an appeal related to the Matter, the Law Firm is not obligated to represent Client(s) in any appeal related to the Matter, and representation on appeal will not commence until Client(s) and the Responsible Attorney have signed a written addendum to this agreement or a separate written agreement dealing with representation on appeal, and any retainer, if applicable to representation on appeal, is in fact paid by Client(s).

Attorney Fees

[Contingency Fee]

Client(s) agree(s) to pay the Law Firm a fee contingent upon the outcome and based upon the recovery received from any party in any file obtained in the Matter. When the term "recovery" is used in this agreement, the term includes any recovery from one or more parties. Thus, if the Matter involves multiple parties and a separate recovery is obtained from more than one party, recovery includes each separate recovery. The recovery is deemed to include all cash, property (tangible and intangible), and any and all other items of value of every type and description which Client(s) receive(s) in this Matter, including but not limited to executory rights. The present value of all items, other than cash, which are included in the recovery, or any partial recovery from any party paying any claim related to the Matter, will be determined for the purpose of calculating the total recovery for use in determining the amount on which the Law Firm's fee is calculated. Unless Client(s) and the Law Firm agree on the amount of all items included in the recovery, other than cash, Client(s) and the Law Firm will share equally in the expense of retaining a duly qualified certified public accountant or other appropriate expert(s) to determine the present value of the items, other than cash, which are included in the recovery. Client(s) shall pay the Law Firm as attorney fees for representation in the Matter according to the following schedule:

1. $33^{1}/_{3}\%$ of the value of all items included in the recovery if the Matter is resolved and settled prior to the beginning of the pretrial conference.
2. 40% of the value of all items included in the recovery if the Matter is resolved and settled after the beginning of the pretrial conference, but before any notice of appeal is filed.
3. 50% of the value of all items included in the recovery if the Matter is resolved after either party files a notice of appeal, petition in error, or other instrument that initiates an appeal, whether the case is presented in a jury or bench trial.

Client(s) authorize(s) the Law Firm to advance the costs and expenses of the Matter, including the costs and expenses of litigation, if applicable, which Client(s) agree(s) to reimburse. All expenses advanced by the Law Firm that have not been previously paid by the Client(s) will be subtracted from Client('s s') portion of any recovery after the Law Firm's fee portion of the recovery is deducted from the amount recovered. If the fees due the Law Firm equal 50% of the recovery, then the costs and expenses will be paid from the Law Firm's portion of the recovery.

In the event of a structured settlement resulting in periodic future payments, all costs and expenses advanced by the Law Firm shall be paid in full before any recovery is paid to Client(s) [or any beneficiary of the Estate] or attorney fees are paid to the Law Firm. After all costs and expenses of the Matter advanced by the Law Firm are paid, each payment on the structured settlement will be divided pro rata between Client(s) and the Law Firm according to the appropriate percentage set out above. In the event no recovery is made, Client(s) will owe no attorney fees. However, Client(s) will be responsible for all costs and expenses incurred in the Matter, regardless of the outcome, even if there is no recovery.

[Hourly Fee]

Client(s) shall pay the Law Firm as attorney fees for representation in the Matter according to the following schedule:

Billing Rates

Billing rates for the Matter are as follows:

- Responsible Attorney $000.00 per hour.
- [Senior/Associate] Attorney $000.00 per hour.
- [Senior/Associate] Attorney $000.00 per hour.
- [Senior/Associate] Attorney $000.00 per hour.
- Law Clerk/Legal Assistant $000.00 per hour.

A minimum of 0.20 hour will be charged for activities performed by the Law Firm and other office personnel assisting with the case, including telephone calls. Client(s) authorize(s) the Law Firm to advance the costs and expenses of the Matter, including the costs and expenses of litigation, if applicable, which Client(s) agree(s) to reimburse.

["RETAINER": OPTIONAL FOR CONTINGENCY OR HOURLY MATTERS]

Retainer

CHOOSE AN OPTION:

1. Client(s) will pay a retainer of $__, which will be deposited in the Law Firm's trust account to be billed against at the hourly rates provided in this agreement. The retainer is payable upon Client('s s') acceptance and return of this agreement to the Law Firm. The Law Firm will bill Client(s) monthly for time, costs, and expenses charged to the Matter. Client(s) shall replenish the retainer each month so that the amount of the original retainer is constantly maintained in the trust account, until the Matter is concluded or until this agreement is terminated. Failure of Client(s) to pay any retainer or replenish any retainer when due will justify the Law Firm's withdrawal from representing Client(s) in the Matter.

2. Client(s) will pay a retainer of $__, which will be deposited in the Law Firm's trust account to be billed against at the hourly rates provided in this agreement. The retainer is payable upon Client('s s') acceptance and return of this agreement to the Law Firm. The Law Firm will bill Client(s) monthly for time, costs, and expenses charged to the Matter. If the retainer is fully expended, the Matter is not concluded, and this agreement is not terminated, Client(s) shall replenish the retainer in the amount of the original retainer, and the Law Firm will bill against the replenished retainer as with the original retainer. Failure of Client(s)

to pay any retainer or replenish any retainer when due will justify the Law Firm's withdrawal from representing Client(s) in the Matter.

3. In the event Client('s s') account becomes past due more than thirty (30) days (i.e., any statement is not paid within thirty (30) days of the statement date), Client(s) will pay a retainer of $__, which will be deposited in the Law Firm's trust account to be billed against at the hourly rates provided in this agreement. The Law Firm will bill Client(s) monthly for time, costs, and expenses charged to the Matter. Client(s) shall replenish the retainer each month so that the amount of the original retainer is constantly maintained in the trust account, until the Matter is concluded or until this agreement is terminated. Client(s) shall continue replenishing the retainer as provided until the Matter is concluded or until this agreement is terminated. Failure of Client(s) to pay any retainer or replenish any retainer when due will justify the Law Firm's withdrawal from representing Client(s) in the Matter.

Billing Statements

[CHOOSE AN OPTION: [1.] FOR CONTINGENCY CASES; [2.] FOR HOURLY FEE CASES.]

[1.] The Law Firm will provide Client(s) a detailed monthly statement for costs and expenses incurred during the month. Each statement will contain an accounting of the charges made to Client('s s') account. All billing statements are due in full upon receipt by Client(s). Client(s) agree(s) to pay, or authorize(s) the Law Firm to pay from the retainer (if applicable), each statement in full upon receipt. Failure to pay any balance when due will justify the Law Firm's withdrawal from representing Client(s) in the Matter.

Each monthly billing cycle begins on the first business day of the month. Any statement not paid in full by the beginning of the next billing cycle is considered past due. For example, a billing statement sent in January for the charges related to the previous December is due upon receipt in January. The January statement would be past due on the first business day in February, which is when the next billing cycle begins.

[2.] The Law Firm will provide Client(s) a detailed monthly statement for attorney fees, costs, and expenses incurred during the month. Each statement will contain an accounting of the charges made to Client('s s') account. All billing statements are due in full upon receipt by Client(s). Client(s) agree(s) to pay, or authorize(s) the Law Firm to pay from the retainer (if applicable), each statement in full upon receipt. Failure to pay any balance when due will justify the Law Firm's withdrawal from representing Client(s) in the Matter.

Each monthly billing cycle begins on the first business day of the month. Any statement not paid in full by the beginning of the next billing cycle is considered past due. For example, a billing statement sent in January for the charges related to the previous December is due upon receipt in January. The January statement would be past due on the first business day in February, which is when the next billing cycle begins.

Interest Charges to Aged Accounts

Any outstanding balances not paid when due as provided in this agreement will accrue an interest charge of eighteen percent [18.0 %] per annum (i.e., one and one-half percent [1.5%] per month) from the due date until paid. Interest charges will apply to the full unpaid balance as shown on the billing statement. Interest charges will continue to accrue until the full balance, including interest, is paid in full. In the event an account becomes past due, payments on the account will be credited first to accrued interest, then to past due balances, then to the current balance due.

Attorney Fee and Cost Cases

Client('s s') Matter may involve a case in which the Court may make an award of attorney fees and/or court costs, if allowed by law. Client(s) agree(s) and acknowledge(s) that Client(s) is/are solely responsible for payment of the Law Firm's, costs, and expenses, even if the Matter is one in which attorney fees and court costs are allowed under law, and even if the Court in fact makes an award to Client(s) for attorney fees and court costs against any opposing party. Client(s) agree(s) and acknowledge(s) that the Matter in which the Law Firm is representing Client(s) does not include or involve any action to collect or recover from any opposing party any award for attorney fees and/or costs if allowed by the Court. OPTION IN CONTINGENCY CASES: [In the event the law allows recovery of attorney fees for the Matter, the attorney fees collected by the Law Firm shall be considered additional attorney fees and will be included in the total amount recovered as part of fees due the Law Firm described above.]

Legal Risks

Client(s) further acknowledge(s) that the Matter is the type of case which may provide for the recovery of attorney fees and/or costs by the prevailing party. Client(s) acknowledge(s) that the Responsible Attorney has fully informed

Client(s) of the legal risk(s) associated with pursuing this matter in connection with the possible award of attorney fees and/or costs to the opposing party in the Matter in the event the opposing party should prevail. Client(s) also acknowledge(s) that the Responsible Attorney has advised Client(s) of all potential risks related to the Matter. Client(s) acknowledge(s) to the Law Firm that Client(s) is/are fully informed and is/are willing to accept the legal risks related to the Matter.

Costs and Expenses

Although the Law Firm may advance costs and expenses of the Matter, Client(s) is/are responsible for all costs and expenses arising out of the investigation, preparation, discovery, and litigation of the Matter, as applicable. The costs of the Matter include, but are not limited to: filing fees, costs of service of process, witness fees (including experts), and deposition costs. The expenses of the Matter include, but are not limited to: postage, photocopy expense, travel, facsimile charges, computer assisted legal research, and long distance telephone calls. Photocopies will be charged at $0.25 per page, and telecopier transmissions/receptions will be charged at $0.25 per page. Fees generated by outside parties will be billed to Client(s) at the same cost the Law Firm is billed.

Legal Insurance

In the event Client(s) has/have any insurance policy that may cover attorney fees, costs, or expenses incurred by Client(s) related to the Matter, this paragraph applies. Payment on Client(s) account is to be made in full by Client(s) on receipt of the statement for the current month. It is Client('s s') responsibility to obtain reimbursement by an insurance company, if applicable. The Law Firm will provide any information, subject to reasonable charges for photocopies, etc., needed to assist Client(s) in filing any claim with an insurance company to recover fees, costs and/or expenses related to the Matter. Client(s) agree(s) to pay all fees, costs, and expenses which are not covered by the Client's insurance policy. Client(s) agree(s) that the Law Firm has not verified that the services provided in this agreement are covered by Client('s s') insurance policy. Further, Client(s) agree(s) that the Law Firm is not responsible for ensuring that the services rendered under this agreement are covered by Client('s s') insurance policy. It shall be Client('s s') sole responsibility to ensure compliance with all terms and conditions of Client('s s') insurance policy.

Attorney's Lien

To the extent allowed and permissible by law and as applicable to this particular Matter, Client(s) agree(s) that the Law Firm has a lien on the claim or cause of action related to the Matter in which Client has an interest, on any sum recovered through settlement or through judgment related to the Matter. The lien is in the amount of the sum and share described in this agreement as attorney fees and shall total the full amount due the Law Firm under this agreement, including the costs and expenses of litigation advanced by the Law Firm. The Law Firm shall have general, possessory, or retaining liens, and all special or charging liens known to common law.

Termination of Agreement

This agreement will terminate upon completion of the Matter described in this agreement. This agreement will also terminate upon withdrawal of the Law Firm, with or without cause, as counsel to Client(s) in this Matter, on reasonable notice to Client(s). In the event of withdrawal, the Law Firm shall retain an attorney's lien for the fee due the Law Firm based upon [**CHOOSE 1. OR 2.: 1. CONTINGENCY CASES:** the quantum merit value of services rendered by the Law Firm in the Matter, in connection with the contingency fee schedule stated above, **2. HOURLY CASES:** the number of hours worked by all attorneys in the Law Firm], and for all costs and expenses the Law Firm has advanced on the Matter. Any balance remaining in the Law Firm's trust account in connection with the Matter will be refunded to Client(s) after an audit of Client('s s') account and payment of any outstanding balance due on the account.

Conflict of Interest

After considering the Responsible Attorney's consultation, Client(s) has/have concluded that no conflict of interest exists or appears imminent which would materially prejudice Client(s) in this Matter, and Client(s) consent(s) to the Law Firm's representation in the Matter. In the event a conflict of interest arises during the course of this representation which cannot be resolved, the Law Firm will withdraw from representation of Client(s) [and/or the Estate] and Client(s) [on behalf of the Estate] shall be liable for all attorney fees, costs, and expenses due in this Matter.

Settlement of case

Client(s) will not make any settlement agreement in this case without the Responsible Attorney's knowledge and consent.

Favorable Outcome Not Warranted

The Law Firm makes no warranties to Client(s) concerning the possible successful outcome of the Matter.

This agreement is signed and effective on the date first written above and at the address for the Law Firm stated above. Client(s) acknowledge(s) receipt of a signed copy of this agreement.

"CLIENT"   [NAME OF CLIENT, IF A COMPANY]

By: [Name of officer or responsible person], [Title]

"LAW FIRM"   [Law Firm]

By:
                            [Lawyer]

Guaranty of Payment of Attorney Fees, Costs, and Expenses

[name of guarantor(s)], [address of guarantor(s)] ("Guarantor(s)"), as the [relationship of guarantor to Client, e.g., parent(s)], of Client(s), agree(s) to pay all attorney fees, costs, and expenses on behalf of Client(s) under this agreement. Guarantor(s) agree(s) to be bound by all of the terms of this agreement in connection with payment of all attorney fees, costs, and expenses incurred in the Matter for which Client(s) is/are responsible.

Guarantor(s) specifically acknowledge(s) and agree(s) that the duty of the Law Firm and Responsible Attorney is solely to Client(s) and not to Guarantor(s), and that the attorney-client relationship is solely between the Law Firm/Responsible Attorney and Client(s), and that no attorney-client relationship exists between the Law Firm/Responsible Attorney and Guarantor(s). Guarantor(s) acknowledge(s) and agree(s) that all decisions made by the Law Firm/Responsible Attorney in connection with the Matter are to be made in connection with Client(s) consent and best interests, without any consideration to Guarantor('s s') preferences.

Guarantor(s) further specifically acknowledge(s) and agree(s) that all client confidences are to be maintained between the Law Firm/Responsible Attorney and will not be disclosed to Guarantor(s) without specific consent of Client(s). Guarantor(s) will not inquire into Client('s s') Matter without specific consent of the Client(s), and Guarantor(s) will not attempt to influence the Law Firm's/Responsible Attorney's decisions concerning representation of Client(s), but that Client(s) shall make all decisions related to the Law Firm's/Responsible Attorney's representation of Client(s) in the Matter.

"GUARANTOR(S)"

[Name of Guarantor]   [Name of Guarantor]

I/We have read this section entitled "Guaranty of Payment of Attorney Fees, Costs, and Expenses," and I/we consent to the agreement of Guarantor(s) to pay on my/our behalf the attorney fees, costs, and expenses incurred in the Matter for which I/we am/are responsible.

"CLIENT"

[Name of Client]

"LAW FIRM"   [Law Firm]

By:

          [Lawyer]

Exhibit

3

Increased Hourly Rate for Negotiations; Contingent Fee if Litigation Is Required

This fee agreement in Exhibit 3 reflects innovative—win-win billing practices. The client, a half owner of a small corporation, had been locked out for years by the other half owner, who controlled the board of directors. When the client came to the law firm, he was cash poor and had been for several years. The corporation had not declared any dividends, and he was not being paid as an employee of the company. Needless to say, the other half owner was living rather well.

The other owner had tried to buy out the client, offering $800,000 to be paid over a long period of time. On the surface, it appeared as if the client's share of the company was worth more than that. The client had tried to get a number of lawyers to represent him on some sort of contingent fee basis. All of them wanted the standard one-third to one-half of any recovery, whether by settlement or litigation. The client felt that he might as well take the $800,000 offered to him, because he would lose so much on attorneys' fees.

The law firm, taking a different approach, offered to charge two and one-half times its regular hourly rates for negotiation services and, if a suitable negotiated settlement could not be achieved, to proceed to litigation when so directed by the client on a standard one-third contingency.

The firm was paid $55,000, two and one-half times its normal hourly rates. The firm was happy; the client was happy to have avoided paying more than $500,000 in attorneys' fees and was overjoyed to receive $1,545,000—almost twice the amount originally offered.

Factors influencing the use of this approach include prior successful litigation by this firm against the other half-owner of the corporation, a preliminary evaluation that the value of the stock was greater than the initial amount offered for the stock, and the reputation of the firm for being vigorous litigators.

Contract of Employment

(Modified Contingency Fee Agreement)

This Contract of Employment is made on December _____, 2007, between [_____], attorneys at law, whose address is [_____], Denver, Colorado 80201 ("counsel") and_____, whose address is _____ ("client").

Recitals

A. Client has requested counsel to provide legal services with respect to _____.

B. To avoid any misunderstanding, client and counsel wish to formalize their agreement regarding employment by this written contract.

C. _____ of our law firm informed _____ of the hourly rates charged by attorneys at this law firm and its policy for charging fees based upon time and other considerations. Instead of that regular fee arrangement, client has requested counsel to provide representation based upon a modified contingency fee arrangement, as further set forth in this agreement.

THEREFORE, client and counsel agree as follows:

1. **Attorneys Fees:** Client agrees to pay counsel a fee contingent upon the outcome of the matter in accordance with the following:
   a. Prior to the filing of litigation, client agrees to pay counsel a fee equal to two and one-half times the regular hourly rate charged by counsel for work done on behalf of its clients. Client has been advised that the regular hourly rates charged by our law firm vary depending upon the level of seniority of the attorneys involved and other factors including the complexity of the work and extraordinary time demands. The regular hourly rate for _____ is presently $_____. Rates for attorneys with a lower level of seniority

are typically lower than this amount and rates for attorneys with higher seniority are typically higher. Regular hourly rates are subject to change from time-to-time in accordance with firm practice.

b. If counsel is directed to bring suit, client agrees to pay counsel a fee equal to $33^1/_3\%$ of all sums recovered by the client as a result of that litigation.

c. Counsel agrees to provide client with regular fee statements and to notify client each time fees reach increments of $5,000, i.e., $5,000, $10,000, etc.

2. **Expenses:** Client acknowledges counsel will incur various expenses in providing services to client. It is understood that client will be responsible for all expenses incurred in this matter regardless of any recovery and will remit those expenses promptly to counsel upon receipt of an invoice. Some examples of these expenses are charges for court filings, depositions, expert witness fees, investigation costs, reports, photocopying, telephone charges, and the costs of hiring accountants to review books and records of _____. If expenses are not remitted promptly upon request, client agrees to pay interest at the annual rate of 18% on all amounts owing more than 30 days.

   Counsel estimates that the expenses involved in this matter may range from approximately $_____ to $_____ but notes that it is unable to make such a prediction with any accuracy because the amount of expenses incurred will necessarily depend upon factors beyond counsel's control, including decisions made by the client, and the efforts of opposing counsel. Client's express approval will be secured for any single expense in excess of $1,000. Furthermore, client's written approval will be secured if and when the expenses exceed $5,000.

3. **Termination of Contract:** Client may terminate this contract by notifying counsel in writing. If permission for withdrawal from employment is required by the rules of any court, counsel shall withdraw upon permission of the court.

   Counsel may withdraw as counsel for client and terminate this contract for any just reason by notifying client in writing. Some examples of reasons for termination include, but are not limited to, client's failure to cooperate with counsel or any request by client which would require counsel to violate the Code of Professional Responsibility approved by the Supreme Court of Colorado.

   If counsel withdraws as client's counsel and terminates this contract, it will take reasonable precautions to avoid any prejudice to the rights of client by allowing a reasonable time for employment of other counsel, delivering to client all papers and property to which client is entitled, and complying with all applicable laws and rules.

If representation is terminated by client or by counsel for any reason, counsel shall be entitled to be compensated at its usual rates in effect as of the date this agreement is signed, but only in the event the client is ultimately successful on the claim or in client's negotiations and receives any amounts from _____or any other defendant.

4. **Miscellaneous**:

This contract contains the entire agreement of client and counsel regarding counsel's employment. This contract shall not be modified or revoked except by written agreement between client and counsel.

This contract shall be binding upon the client and counsel and their heirs, executors, legal representatives, successors and assigns.

This contract shall be construed and governed by the laws of the State of Colorado.

In the event of litigation or arbitration concerning this contract, reasonable fees and costs shall be awarded to the prevailing party.

Client acknowledges having read this contract in its entirety and declares it to be fair and reasonable.

CLIENTCOUNSEL

[_____]

[_____]

Denver, CO 80201

303-[_____]

_____   By: _____

Date: _____   Date: _____

Exhibit

4

Alternative Billing Proposal for Either Hourly Rates or Reduced Hourly Rates with a Contingency Fee if the Business Is Acquired

The following form has been used by a Houston law firm when clients desired to acquire a business. The law firm agreed to work on either a normal hourly basis or, if the acquisition is abandoned or not consummated before a prescribed date, accept a defined percent of the normal fees. If the percent fee is paid promptly, the balance of accrued time is forgiven.

If the acquisition is consummated, a fee at the normal hourly rate will be paid, with all or a portion of the fee evidenced by an interest-bearing note in quarterly installments. As an inducement to use the firm's services after closing, the firm will forgive up to one-half of the principal amount of the note in an amount equal to 50 percent of the fees collected from legal services rendered by the firm to the acquiring corporation within one year after the time of the closing.

For example, assume the principal amount of the note is $100,000, and within one year after the closing, the acquiring corporation pays the firm $50,000 in legal fees before making any principal payments. In that case, the principal amount of the note will be reduced to $75,000 ($50,000 X 50% with a cap of 50 percent of the then unpaid principal amount of the note = $25,000).

This arrangement has worked well where prospective entrepreneurs are attempting an acquisition that seems sound, the lawyers are willing to share risks and are willing to make concessions initially with the hope that the acquisition will be consummated, and the acquiring corporation will continue to use the legal services of the firm after closing.

It demonstrates that the choice of a billing method, some risk sharing, and some recognition of the economic needs of the clients can be tools for developing new clients—the gamble being that the acquisition will be consummated, that the business acquired will be successful, and that the company will continue to use the services of the firm.

Fee Agreement

Personal & Confidential

ABC Client
Success Tower
Houston, Texas
Gentlemen:

The purpose of this letter is to summarize our understanding with respect to the engagement of [_____] (the "Firm") in connection with the acquisition (the "Acquisition") by you and the individuals who have executed the last page of this agreement (collectively, the "Acquirers") of Target Corporation (the "Company"). The engagement will involve (i) conferences with, among others, the Acquirers, the Company's officers, directors, investment bankers and independent certified accountants; (ii) the review and/or preparation of documents to evidence the Acquisition of the Company; and (iii) such other services that are necessary.

Our agreement with respect to the engagement is as follows:

(a) The hourly rates we charge for legal services range from $200 to $300 per hour for all time expended by principals of the Firm, $90 to $175 per hour for associates and $50 to $70 per hour for legal assistants. I will be responsible on a day-to-day basis for the supervision of the representation in connection with matters such as the Acquisition. Other attorneys who probably will render legal services in connection with this matter are [_____] and [_____], whose hourly billing rates are $225 and $175, respectively. The determination of whether a principal, an associate or a legal assistant renders services to you depends upon the nature of the work and the qualifications of the person needed to perform that particular aspect of the engagement. Attached hereto as Exhibit "A" is a list of the hourly billing rates you will be charged for the Firm's attorneys and legal assistants.

(b) We estimate that legal fees in connection with this representation will range from approximately $100,000 to $125,000. While we will endeavor to keep the fees to a minimum, please recognize that this estimate is merely a rough approximation based upon our prior experience, and the ultimate fees may vary depending upon the actual facts and the services rendered in connection with the engagement. Should it appear that the legal fees will be in excess of the estimate, you will be notified as soon as practicable.

(c) Prior to calling on the Firm to render services, you and the Acquirers will unanimously agree as to the manner by which we will be paid for such services. The two alternatives we are willing to accept are described in Exhibit "B." On the last page of this agreement, either Alternative A or Alternative B has been marked by you and the Acquirers, and the parties agree to be jointly and severally bound by the terms of this agreement and that Alternative.

On a monthly basis, the Firm will furnish you and the Acquirers detailed invoices of the services rendered and the amount of fees and reimbursable disbursements (including, but not limited to, filing fees, parking fees, overtime charges for secretarial services, copying costs, and long-distance telephone charges) incurred on your behalf. Overtime charges for secretarial services will only be charged if the hiring of one or more secretaries is necessary in order to meet deadlines. The invoices will explain in detail the nature and date of the services rendered and reimbursable expenses. If you or any of the Acquirers do not agree with the charges set forth on the invoices, I will be notified within two weeks of receipt of the invoices. If I am not notified that there is a question or that someone disagrees with the charges, it will be irrebuttably presumed that the charges are fair and reasonable.

(d) If the Firm's invoices are not paid when due, you and the Acquirers will also be billed the standard hourly rates for all time expended by the Firm's attorneys in the Firm's collection efforts and $25 per hour for all administrative time expended in collection efforts. Furthermore, you and the Acquirers will also be responsible for all expenses incurred in connection with the collection of amounts due to the Firm, including fees of attorneys who are not employees of the Firm, should such collection efforts become necessary.

(e) This agreement shall be construed in accordance with the laws of the State of Texas and all obligations of the parties are performable in Harris County, Texas. This agreement shall be binding upon and inure to the benefit of the parties and their respective heirs, executors, administrators, legal representatives, successors and assigns.

(f) In case any one or more of the provisions contained shall be held to be invalid, illegal or unenforceable in any respect, such invalidity, illegality or unenforceability shall not affect any other provision, and this agreement shall be construed as if such invalid, illegal or unenforceable provision did not exist.

(g) Once executed, this agreement constitutes the only agreement of the parties with respect to matters involving the engagement of the Firm, the payment of fees in connection therewith, and supersedes any prior understandings or written or oral agreements between the parties respecting such subject matter.

(h) This agreement may be executed in multiple counterparts, each of which shall be deemed an original, but all of which shall constitute one and the same instrument.

Gentlemen, I apologize for the formal tone of this agreement, but it is important that we fully understand what is expected of one another. Therefore, if this letter accurately sets forth the agreement as to the basis upon which the Firm has been engaged, please have this agreement signed and return the signed copy to me. The second copy is for your records.

We are looking forward to working with you on this matter and anticipate a long and mutually beneficial relationship.

Very truly yours,

[_____]

[_____]

AGREED AND ACCEPTED this day of _____, 200__.
ABC Client
    By:
        (Name Printed)   (Title)

Also, the undersigned jointly and severally agree to (i) be bound by the terms of this agreement; (ii) the Alternative marked below; and (iii) pay any amounts due to the Firm hereunder pursuant to the terms of this agreement.
[ ] Alternative A
[ ] Alternative B
(Name Printed)   (Name Printed)

Exhibit "A"

Hourly Billing Rates from October 1, 2007, through September 30, 2008

Hourly
Billing Rate

Principals
Associates
Legal Assistants

Exhibit "B"

Alternative A

The Firm's invoices are due upon presentment. The invoice for services in a particular month is usually mailed between the 10th and 15th day of the following month (the "Month of Receipt"). Any invoice that is not paid by the first day of the month following the Month of Receipt will bear interest at the rate of eighteen percent (18%) per annum commencing on the first day of the month following the Month of Receipt. For example, an invoice for fees and out-of-pocket expenditures for March 2008 will be mailed between April 10 and April 15. If such invoice is not paid in full by May 1, 2008, interest will accrue on the unpaid amount commencing May ___, 2008.

Alternative B

In the event the Acquisition is abandoned or not consummated on or before August 31, 200__ (the earlier to occur of either abandonment or August 31, 200__ being the "Termination Date"), the Acquirers will pay the Firm within 14 days of the Termination Date (the "Payment Date") an amount equal to the aggregate of the out-of-pocket disbursements incurred by the Firm through the Termination Date. In addition to the foregoing, on the Payment Date you and the Acquirers will pay the Firm an amount equal to ___% of the legal fees incurred in connection with the Acquisition. If the firm receives on or before the Payment Date the amount you and the Acquirers owe the Firm, the remaining ___% of the fees incurred will be forgiven and you the Acquirers will have no liability therefor. However, if such payment is not received on or before the Payment Date, you and the Acquirers will remain responsible for all legal fees rendered in addition to any charges arising pursuant to paragraph (d) of the agreement to which this Exhibit "B" is attached.

In the event the Acquisition is consummated (the "Closing"), the aggregate amount (legal fees and out-of-pocket disbursements) set forth on the Firm's invoices to you the Acquirers will be paid at the time of the Closing plus any fees not covered by the following described Note. In addition to paying the Firm the amounts set forth on the Firm's invoices at the time of the Closing, at that time you and the Acquirers will execute and deliver to the Firm a promissory note (the "Note") in an amount equal to ___% of the amount of legal fees incurred through the day of Closing. The Note will (i) provide for the payment of interest at 10% per annum; and (ii) be payable monthly with four equal quarterly payments of principal, each in an amount equal to 25% of the original principal amount of the Note. In addition, you and the Acquirers and any corporation(s) and/or partnership(s) that are organized for the Acquisition or acquired in connection therewith (collectively, the "Acq. Corp.") shall be a maker of such Note. The Note shall be substantially in the form attached hereto as Exhibit "__."

As an inducement for you and the Acquirers to utilize the Firm's services after the time of the Closing, the Firm will forgive up to one-half of the principal amount of the Note in an amount equal to 50% of the fees collected from legal services rendered by the Firm to the Acq. Corp. within one year subsequent to the time of the Closing. It is acknowledged that such credit will be based upon collections, not billings, received by the Firm within one year from the time of the Closing.

For example, if the principal amount of the Note is $100,000 and, within one year subsequent to the Closing, the Acq. Corp. pays the Firm $50,000 in legal fees before any principal payments are made, the principal amount of the Note will be reduced to $75,000 ($50,000 X 50% with a cap of 50% of the then unpaid principal amount of the Note = $25,000).

Any amount that is not paid when due under this Alternative B, either at the time of the Closing or the Termination Date, will bear interest at the rate of eighteen percent (18%) per annum commencing on the first day of the month following the due date. In addition, you and the Acquirers will be responsible for the charges arising pursuing to paragraph (d) of the agreement to which this Exhibit "__" is attached.

Exhibit

5

Agreement for Fixed Fee Representation of a Bank for Major Collection Litigation with Bonus Clause

The innovative fee agreement in Exhibit 5 was used starting in 1989 with a large firm where the bank was instituting suits to recover unpaid indebtedness. This agreement may soon be used in cases where the bank is a defendant or is defending a counterclaim.

Initially, the bank entered into an agreement with the law firm to have a test period with 10 lawsuits where the bank was suing one or more entities legally liable for indebtedness. The law firm and the bank both kept detailed records of the amount of time spent in resolving those 10 cases, after which the parties mutually analyzed this information. During this initial experimental stage, it was agreed that for the legal services rendered in each of the 10 cases, the bank would pay the lesser of the fixed fee pursuant to the contract or the actual time value billing based on an hourly rate. No bonus amount would be involved for the 10 test cases, unless the bank felt that it was warranted.

Ten months after the beginning of these test cases, seven had been resolved to the bank's satisfaction. Of those seven cases, five resulted in the contractual fixed fee being less than the usual hourly rate calculation. The bank's analysis showed that these cases were resolved significantly faster than the cases handled by the same firm under the previous straight hourly fee system. Additionally, the law firm indicated that its revenues from the bank group significantly increased over this shorter time period. In short, both the bank and the law firm believed they had received value from this arrangement. The law firm and the bank plan to continue using this method to handle more cases.

From the law firm's standpoint, the most important element of this type of arrangement is a volume of cases. The law firm is willing to accept the risk of underestimating what it might actually take to resolve some of these disputes only if it is relatively assured that a number of other cases will be referred to the firm to serve as opportunities to compensate for any losses.

Internally, the bank's analysis of this arrangement indicated that using this method led to a proportionate reduction in the bank's overall outside litigation expense, as well as reducing the bank's person-hours and "time value" savings of money, since these matters were resolved faster than normal.

Note that the agreement specifies the characteristics of the cases that will be handled. There is a range stipulating a minimum and maximum amount in controversy. The law firm can reject a prescribed number of cases. The services to be performed are set forth, as are the services that are excluded, with the proviso that any excluded services under the fee agreement will be performed by the law firm for an hourly fee.

If an eligible claim is resolved quickly, the law firm is entitled to a bonus computed on an agreed-upon percentage of the amount in controversy.

If the services provided are satisfactory, the bank agrees to meaningfully consider engaging the firm for other legal representation, such as litigation of noneligible claims and business transactions. Under this agreement, the bank commits to providing a volume of business, with the prospect of more to come. The bank's interest in speedy resolution is met by the incentive for the bonus. Both the fixed fee aspect and the bonus provision provide an incentive for the law firm to be efficient.

The innovation demonstrated by this corporate counsel in setting up this type of arrangement is admirable. The agreement certainly seems to be another win-win billing method.

Agreement for Fixed Fee Representation

_____ agrees to represent
_____ ("Client") and Client hereby engages
_____ to represent Client in defense
of Eligible Claims (defined herein) upon the following terms and conditions:

1. **Definitions.** As used herein, "Eligible Claims" means those claims (whether asserted by formal petition, complaint or application or pleading before any judicial or administrative entity) against Client which are frequently recurring and generally identified by common characteristics, such as the following:

   (a) All legal claims for relief by one plaintiff, or common claims by multiple (but not more than ____) plaintiffs acting in a community of interest, i.e., spouses, partners, etc., asserted in a separate proceeding identified by a case, cause or proceeding number;

   (b) Claims arising out of the same transaction or series of transactions between plaintiffs and Client;

   (c) Claims in which the amount of alleged unliquidated damages in controversy is not less than $_____ and does not exceed $_____; and

   (d) [Other common characteristics to be determined by Client and _____].

   "Client" means _____ and any related persons or entities named as defendant(s) in the proceedings who have or hold a common interest in defense of the Eligible Claims, such as parent or subsidiary corporations, directors, officers and employees, provided that representation of_____, its parent or subsidiary corporations, or its directors, officers or employees would or does not constitute an ethical conflict of interest.

2. **Term.** This agreement commences as of _____, 2008, and shall terminate on _____, 200__.

3. **Referral of Eligible Claims.** Client shall refer for legal representation all matters which are or may constitute Eligible Claims and which are served upon Client during the term of this agreement. In order to compensate for any disagreements as to whether a matter constitutes an Eligible Claim, _____ may decline to undertake representation of Client in as many as _____ such matters (exclusive of ethical conflicts), in which event Client is free to engage other legal counsel.

4. **Flat Fee.** Upon referral of each Eligible Claim matter, Client shall pay _____ $_____ as a fee ("the Flat Fee") for the legal services, described herein, associated with the particular Eligible Claim.

5. **Legal Services.** Upon referral and undertaking of representation of Client with respect to Eligible Claims of a plaintiff, _____ shall represent Client with professional zeal and diligence and in a manner which, at a minimum, complies with the letter and spirit of the Texas Code of Professional Responsibility. Except as stated in paragraph 6

of this agreement, _____ shall provide all legal services reasonably necessary to resolve, settle and terminate the Eligible Claims and to defend Client from the date that the Eligible Claims are referred to _____ through the trial and any post-trial proceedings. Except as specified in paragraph 11 of this agreement or otherwise agreed, _____ representation of Client in each separate matter shall terminate on the day that is the earlier of the date that (1) the Eligible Claims are dismissed by mutual request of plaintiff(s) and Client or (2) an appeal bond, if any, is filed by plaintiff(s) or Client.

The legal services which _____ shall provide, as necessary, include but are not limited to the following:

(a) Pleadings;

(b) Motions and responses to plaintiff(s)'s motions, if any;

(c) Fact investigation and discovery, including depositions, witness interviews, interrogatories, document production requests and requests for admissions;

(d) Legal research;

(e) Client consultation, including status reports, strategy formulation and advice;

(f) Hearings upon pre-trial motions and applications;

(g) Trial of the Eligible Claims;

(h) Settlement negotiation and communication;

(i) Simple settlement agreements (which contemplate full performance of all terms upon closing of the settlement); and

(j) Termination of any litigation via order of dismissal or final judgment.

6. **Services Not Encompassed by Flat Fee.** The following services related to the Eligible Claims are expressly excluded from the scope of _____ representation pursuant to this agreement:

(a) Prosecution of any counterclaim(s) by Client against plaintiff(s);

(b) Negotiation, drafting and preparation of agreements which contemplate a continued relationship between Client and plaintiff(s) or future performance by either party (i.e., restructured loans, payout of settlement amounts, etc.);

(c) Appeals by either Client or plaintiff(s) including interim appeals or requests for appellate court review of pretrial orders (such as by mandamus, etc.);

(d) [other].

If requested by Client, _____ will provide legal representation to Client with respect to any of such excluded matters. Unless agreed otherwise, _____ shall provide and Client will pay for such representation based upon normal hourly rates of the _____ attorneys providing such legal services.

7. **Client Cooperation.** Client recognizes, acknowledges, and approves of _____ intention, and authorizes _____ to cause prompt settlement and resolution of Eligible Claims and prompt termination of any litigation arising therefrom. Client shall provide all assistance necessary to accomplish prompt settlement and resolution of Eligible Claims and related litigation, including the following:

    (a) Provide factual information deemed relevant by _____;
    (b) Advance necessary expenses;
    (c) Participate in good faith in settlement discussions or events such as alternative dispute resolution methods (arbitrations, mediations, etc.) and informal settlement communication with plaintiff(s) or plaintiff(s)'s attorneys; and
    (d) Timely perform all obligations undertaken pursuant to a binding settlement agreement with plaintiff(s).

8. **Expenses.** Client shall pay _____ all reasonably necessary out-of-pocket expenses advanced in connection with the representation and legal services provided with respect to Eligible Claims. Such expenses shall be identified upon monthly statements by itemized description, such as photocopying, long-distance telephone charges, travel, secretarial overtime (including paralegals), supplies, expert witnesses, court costs, depositions, etc. Where any single expense item exceeds $200, such as a court reporter's statement for depositions, _____ may forward such statements to Client and same shall be promptly paid by Client directly to the vendor.

9. **Bonus.** _____ shall be entitled to add to the final statement related to any specific Eligible Claims and to be paid a bonus if the Eligible Claims are resolved to Client's satisfaction in no later than _____ months from the day of their referral to _____. Resolution of the Eligible Claims shall be evidenced by a written agreement signed by Client and plaintiff(s). The amount of the bonus shall be ____ % of the "amount in controversy" in the proceeding in which the Eligible Claims are asserted. The "amount in controversy" shall be established by agreement of Client and _____.

10. **Representation of Client in Other Legal Matters.** If Client is satisfied with _____ representation and legal services with respect to Eligible Claims, Client will meaningfully consider engaging to provide legal representation in other matters requiring such services, such as litigation of non-Eligible Claims, business transactions, etc.

11. **Termination of Representation.** Client may terminate _____ representation of Client with respect to any Eligible Claims upon reasonable notice. If ____ representation is terminated (by Client, disqualification or withdrawal necessary under the circumstances) before such representation would otherwise naturally terminate by resolution or disposition of the Eligible Claims, then _____ shall be paid the value of legal services performed and expenses incurred to the date of termination of such representation, but in no event more than the Flat Fee.

SIGNED this _____ day of _____, 200__.
   "Client"

                By:

                Its _____

                By:

                Vice President

Exhibit

6

Fixed Fee Corporation Representation Service Election Form

Exhibit 6 is the election form for a corporate client to elect certain services to be provided at a fixed fee by a service agent company established by a law firm to act in that capacity. The service is discussed in Chapter 5, dealing with technology and in the case study for the Corporate Representation Services found in this Appendix.

Corporate Representation Services, LLC

Business Compliance Solutions

Corporate Representation Services, LLC was established to provide business compliance solutions for private companies—ensuring that the necessary legal formalities are met and providing service agent, corporate meeting and stock transfer services to our clients. With special updates and reminders, we keep our clients abreast of new legal developments that might affect private businesses.

For a single annual fee of $150 for each legal entity, we provide corporations and limited liability companies with the following basic services:

- Prepare standard annual meeting minutes for shareholders and directors of corporations or members of limited liability companies.

- Act as the Oklahoma service agent for the company.
- Provide an annual company audit and compliance questionnaire used to identify compliance issues and keep the corporate records accurate and current.
- Prepare a company profile reflecting the current owners and management in addition to other key legal business items.
- Make available conference room facilities for meetings.

Additional services are provided at a reasonable cost to our clients, including private company stock transfer services, director and member packets and guidebooks, and special assistance in preparing shareholder agreements, dependent care assistance and medical reimbursement plans, stock option and other benefit programs.

ELECTION: **[Organization]**

❑ **Yes**—I elect to continue the Corporate Representation Service for [Organization] and wish you to prepare the necessary meeting minutes for [Years Due].

❑ Please check if there have been no changes since last year and the accompanying profile information is correct.

❑ **No**—I do not wish to continue the Corporate Representation Service for [Organization]; please remove this company from the service.

If you would like to receive your minutes and other corporate documents electronically, please check below and list your e-mail address.

❑ I would like to receive my information electronically. My e-mail address is:

MAIL OR FAX RESPONSE PLEASE: Fax Number [_____]

Exhibit

7

Fixed Fee Retainer Agreement for Handling Insurance Defense Cases Based on a Prescribed Volume of Cases

The law firm and the insurance company that signed the retainer agreement in Exhibit 7 agreed that for a period of two years, based on a caseload of 180 cases, the law firm would defend all cases in four contiguous counties for a fixed annual fee payable in monthly installments. The duties of the law firm and the insurance company are set forth. If trials run more than 10 trial days, additional compensation would be paid on an hourly basis. If the caseload drops below the prescribed 180 cases, the agreement can be modified at prescribed times. Also, either party can terminate the agreement on giving 60 days' notice.

**RETAINER AGREEMENT BETWEEN THE LAW FIRM OF
_____ AND _____ INSURANCE CO.**

This is a 2-year Retainer Agreement entered into between the _____ Insurance Co. (Company) and the law firm of _____ (Law Firm) to become effective on the 1st day of January, 20___, and to continue until the last day of December, 20___.

Whereas, the Company is desirous of having the Law Firm represent it in certain areas on a retainer basis and the Law Firm is desirous of representing the Company, the following terms will be applicable to this Agreement.

The following is a list of some of the major items that the Law Firm will obligate itself to perform pursuant to this Agreement:

1. To maintain in force during the life of this 2-year Retainer Agreement a policy of malpractice insurance, with limits of not less than One Million Dollars ($1,000,000.00).
2. To receive and handle lawsuits received from the Company in _____ Counties.
3. To provide opinions on coverage or cases not in suit.
4. To prepare and file declaratory judgment actions.
5. This Retainer Agreement does not include filing of subrogation suits in automobile or fire cases.
6. While not inclusive of all the handling of such suits, the following list will cover the major activities with respect to the handling of such suits:
    A. To send the Company a written acknowledgment of each suit file received;
    B. To prepare and timely file all responsive pleadings in the suits;
    C. To take all necessary depositions and to provide a summary of the contents of the same to the Company;
    D. To generally handle all the activities involved in defending suits including, but not limited to, all court calls, motions, hearings, pretrials, and such;
    E. To conduct trial whenever requested by the Company. This Retainer covers a trial of 2 weeks (10 actual trial days) after which, if the trial continues, the Law Firm will be paid for the remainder of the trial time at its current hourly rate; except on cases tried by _____ the retainer covers 7 actual trial days after which, if the trial continues, the Law Firm will be paid for the remainder of the trial time at its current hourly rate;
    F. To make written status reports to the Company regarding all such suits. The initial opinion letter is to be sent to the Company within 45 days of the assignment and written status reports shall be made at no less than 90-day intervals unless otherwise agreed;
    G. To provide legal opinions and analysis to Company personnel upon request, both on cases in suit and on cases not yet in suit, but falling within the categories set forth above;
    H. To handle any necessary post-trial motions;

I. To be available for consultation or conference with claims personnel of the Company;

J. To arrange for the proper termination of suits by filing of the necessary documents and making a final report to the Company; and

K. To negotiate settlement of claims in suits when requested by the Company but not to settle cases under any circumstances without prior approval from the Company.

In consideration for the services rendered by the Law Firm, the Company will pay the Law Firm the sum of _____ Dollars ($_____) per year in the following manner:

_____ Thousand Dollars ($_____) per month paid on the first day of each month this Agreement is in effect.

In addition to the amount listed above, the Company agrees to pay all of the expenses incurred in the handling of such suits including, but not limited to, the following:

1. Court reporter bills, court costs, appearance fees, subpoena fees, witness fees, photocopy expenses, reproduction of records expenses, and any other approved expenses incurred and allocated to the handling of the suit;

2. Long-distance telephone call expenses incurred in the course of handling such suits.

It is further agreed between the parties that the final decision to appeal a lawsuit will be made by the Company. If the Company decides that an appeal is to be taken, the Company will pay additional sums for the attorneys' fees for the handling of the appeal based either upon a flat dollar amount or upon an hourly rate to be agreed upon by the parties. The Company will bear all of the costs and expenses with respect to the appeal.

The Company further agrees that it will photostat its files and forward originals to the Law Firm for its use in the defense of suits.

This Agreement may be terminated by either party on 60 days' prior written notice of termination. If the 2-year Retainer Agreement is terminated by either party, the Law Firm agrees to immediately return all suit files in its possession, including attorneys' work product, to the Company and agrees to a substitution of Attorneys on such pending suits. The Law Firm further agrees to cooperate fully in an orderly transfer of such suits from its control and to protect the interests of the Company and the Company's insureds in doing so. Payment of the 2-year Retainer fees by the Company will cease as of the effective date of termination. The Law Firm agrees not to file any Attorney's Liens on suits transferred to other attorneys.

It is anticipated that, and this Retainer Agreement has been entered into with the belief of the parties that, it will involve approximately 180 files.

Executed this ___day of _____ , 20__.

"Company"   _____ INSURANCE COMPANY

                                             By: _____

"Law Firm"   _____

                                             By: _____

Exhibit

8

Fee Agreement Incorporating Hourly, Fixed and Unit Fees for a Real Estate Development Project

The following innovative fee proposal to a real estate developer covers several alternative billing methods—discounted hourly rates, maximum fees, fixed fees, and unit fees based upon an agreed unit rate per square foot. See also the case study covering this alternative fee arrangement in this Appendix.

A Sample Fee Proposal for Real Estate Development

We are pleased to present XYZ Limited Partnership (the **"Client"**) with this fee proposal in connection with the Client's efforts to develop [retail center] and [office park] (together, the **"Project"**) in the Village of Arcadia. Our understanding of the Project is based on the [dated site plan] prepared by Design Group.

Fee Structures Defined

In discussing our legal services fees, this proposal incorporates the terms **"Discounted Hourly Fee," "Maximum Fee," "Fixed Fee,"** and **"Unit Fee."** What we mean by these terms is the following:

Discounted Hourly Fee means a total fee calculated by multiplying an agreed hourly services rate by the total number of hours devoted to the applicable matter. Each of the lawyers on our practice team is assigned a standard hourly services rate, which we have set forth on the attached Exhibit A. The hourly services rates we propose for the Project, however, have been reduced from the standard rates we would expect to charge for such a development. These rates are also shown on Exhibit A.

Maximum Fee means a total fee calculated by multiplying an agreed hourly services rate by the total number of hours devoted to the applicable matter, provided that the total fee shall not exceed a specified maximum amount. In this instance, the hourly service rate shall be the Discounted Hourly Rate set forth on Exhibit A.

Fixed Fee means a specified fee payable by the Client without regard to the number of service hours devoted to the pertinent matter.

Unit Fee means a total fee calculated by multiplying an agreed unit rate by the total number of units involved in the applicable matter. In this instance, Unit Fees are established for certain leasing matters based on the rentable square footage of the demised premises.

Fee Breakdown: [retail center]

We understand that the Client's plans for [retail center], the retail portion of the Project, call for development of three anchor pads (one each for a home improvement store, food center, and department store), eight outlots (including one each for a drug store, fast-food restaurant, and bank), and from 25,000 to 45,000 square feet of in-line retail space. We propose to provide legal services for this part of the Project on the following bases:

REA and Project Planning—Discounted Hourly Fee. *Team Members: Adams, Brown, and Carter.* A substantial effort will be required to lay the Project's groundwork. This effort obviously must include defining and establishing the Project's tax parcels, determining its common areas, and drafting and negotiating—and, as development goes forward, amending—the controlling reciprocal easement agreement. Laying the groundwork for the Project must also include preparing standard documentation (such as standard purchase and sale agreements, ground leases, in-line retail leases, and letters of intent) for use in connection with prospective buyers, tenants, and lenders.

We will provide services in connection with drafting the Reciprocal Easement Agreement (REA) and with addressing the general planning tasks we have identified, as well as others as they arise, at the Discounted Hourly Fee.

Adams will be the Client's principal contact for all REA and project planning matters. He will be assisted in REA matters and in preparing anchor tenant agreements by Brown. In the balance of the project planning matters (including establishing tax parcels, preparing other forms of agreement, and all other planning efforts), Adams will be assisted by Carter.

Financing—Fixed Fee to be agreed based on the Client's determination of financing arrangements. *Team Members: Adams, Brown, Davis, and Ellis.* Client plans to develop the Project in phases. This phased development will call for a number of different credit facilities. Right now, however, the outlines of the required credit transactions remain subject to a considerable number of variables, including the number and location of the Project's tax parcels, the identity of the retail anchor tenants and the nature of their realty interest in the Project, and the Client's specific plans for phasing the projected retail and office portions of the development.

We are confident that our services in connection with the required financings can be provided on a Fixed Fee basis for each such financing transaction. We are also confident that we can reach agreement with the Client on the terms of such Fixed Fee arrangements as the key details of the Project emerge with greater clarity. Alternatively, such services—whether uniformly or on a financing-by-financing basis—could also be provided at the Discounted Hourly Rate.

In any event, Adams will be the Client's principal contact for all financing matters. We expect that he will be regularly assisted by Davis, a partner in our real estate practice group who specializes in lending matters—especially in construction lending. Carter and Legal Assistant would assist Adams and Davis as required, particularly in addressing title, title insurance, and survey matters.

Anchor Pad Sales and Ground Leasing—Maximum Fee. *Team Members: Brown, Carter, and Legal Assistant.* For anchor pad sales and ground leases ultimately consummated with a purchaser or ground lessee, services will be charged per transaction based on the Discounted Hourly Fee, up to a maximum total fee of $[_] per sale and $[_] per ground lease. Services rendered in transactions not ultimately consummated will also be billed at the Discounted Hourly Rate, but the total invoice for any unconsummated transaction will not exceed the specified Maximum Fee.

Brown will be the Client's principal contact for all anchor pad ground leases and Carter will be the Client's principal contact for all anchor pad sales. Legal Assistant will help prepare sale and, where practical, leasing documentation.

Anchor Tenant Build-to-Suit Leases—Unit Fee. *Team members: Brown and Carter.* For original build-to-suit leases ultimately executed by an anchor tenant, services will be provided at a Unit Fee per transaction of [_]¢ per rentable square foot of the leased space. Rentable square footage will be determined according to the rentable area figure (calculated by the prevailing Building Owners and Managers Association (BOMA) standard) specified in the controlling lease.

Services rendered in preparing lease amendments, lease renewals, lease assignments, and subleases will be billed at the Discounted Hourly Rate. Services rendered in transactions not ultimately consummated will also be billed at the Discounted Hourly Rate, but the total invoice will not exceed the Unit Fee that would have been owing had the lease been executed.

Brown will be the Client's principal contact for all anchor build-to-suit leasing. Brown and Carter together will be responsible for preparing lease documentation.

Outparcel Sales and Ground Leasing—Maximum Fee. *Team Members: Brown, Carter, and Legal Assistant.* For outparcel sales and ground leases ultimately consummated with a purchaser or ground lessee, services will be charged per transaction based on the Discounted Hourly Fee, up to a maximum total fee of $[_] per sale or ground lease to a local tenant and $[_] per ground lease to a national tenant. (National tenants include all chain and franchise entities and their affiliates; local tenants include all other entities.) Services rendered in transactions not ultimately consummated will also be billed at the Discounted Hourly Rate, but the total invoice for any unconsummated transaction will not exceed the specified Maximum Fee.

Brown will be the Client's principal contact for all outparcel ground leases and Carter will be the Client's principal contact for all outparcel sales. Legal Assistant will help prepare sale and, where practical, leasing documentation.

In-line Retail Leasing—Unit Fee. *Team Members: Carter and Legal Assistant.* For original leases ultimately executed by both landlord and tenant, services will be provided based on a Unit Fee calculated per transaction based on the rentable square footage of each leased space. Unit Fees will be [_]¢ per rentable square foot for national tenants and [_]¢ per rentable square foot for local tenants. Rentable square footage will be determined according to the rentable area figure (calculated by the prevailing BOMA method) specified in the controlling lease.

Services rendered in preparing lease amendments, lease renewals, lease assignments, and subleases will be billed at the Discounted Hourly Rate. Services rendered in transactions not ultimately consummated will also be billed at the Discounted Hourly Rate, but the total invoice will not exceed the Unit Fee that would have been owing had the lease been executed.

Carter will be the Client's principal contact for all in-line leasing. Carter and Legal Assistant together will be responsible for preparing lease documentation

Fee Breakdown: [office park]

We understand that the Client's plans for [office park], the office park portion of the Project, call for the development of six sites suitable to accommodate Class A office uses. We propose to provide legal services for this part of the Project on the following bases:

REA and Project Planning—Discounted Hourly Fee. *Team Members: Adams and Carter.* As noted in our remarks on the REA and project planning for the retail portion of the Project, we will provide services in connection with the office park REA (including, in addition to the same issues arising with the retail spaces, organizing and documenting an owners association) and general office park planning on the basis of the Discounted Hourly Fee. Again, Adams will be the Client's principal contact for all REA and project planning matters. He will be assisted in office park REA and project planning matters by Carter.

Financing—Fixed Fee to be agreed based on the Client's determination of financing arrangements. *Team Members: Adams, Davis, Carter, and Legal Assistant.* Servicing in connection with financing transactions required for the office portion of the Project will be provided on the same basis as with the retail portion of the Project—that is, on the basis of a Fixed Fee to be negotiated as the Client's plans solidify or on the basis of a Discounted Hourly Fee. Again, Adams and Davis will be the Client's principal contacts for all financing matters, with Carter and Legal Assistant assisting in title, title insurance, and survey matters.

Parcel Sales and Ground Leasing—Fixed Fee. *Team Members: Carter and Legal Assistant.* For office parcel sales and ground leases ultimately consummated with a purchaser or ground lessee, services will be charged per transaction based on a Fixed Fee of $[_] per sale or ground lease. Services rendered in any transaction not ultimately consummated will be billed at the Discounted Hourly Rate, but the total invoice for an unconsummated transaction will not exceed the specified Fixed Fee.

Carter will be the Client's principal contact for all office parcel ground leases and sales. Legal Assistant will help prepare sale and, where practical, leasing documentation.

Office Build-to-Suit Leases. *Team Member: Carter.* For original build-to-suit leases ultimately executed by an office park tenant, services will be provided at a Unit Fee per transaction of [_]¢ per rentable square foot of the leased space. Rentable square footage will be determined according to the rentable area figure (calculated by the prevailing BOMA method) specified in the controlling lease.

Services rendered in preparing lease amendments, lease renewals, lease assignments, and subleases will be billed at the Discounted Hourly Rate. Services rendered in transactions not ultimately consummated will also be billed at the Discounted Hourly Rate, but the total invoice will not exceed the Unit Fee that would have been owing had the lease been executed.

Carter will be the Client's contact for all office park build-to-suit leasing.

Construction Contracting

As indicated in our original presentation to the Client, Ellis of our office will be the project team member responsible for all construction contracting matters. This includes review of all AIA and AGC agreements and handling of all lien, contracting, and subcontracting matters. Charges for services rendered in connection with construction contracting matters will be billed at the Discounted Hourly Fee.

Other Matters

Matters not outlined in this proposal will be handled by project team members where appropriate. In other instances—for example, environmental matters, state regulatory matters, and *ad valorem* tax assessment contests arising in connection with the Project—we will propose other members of the firm whose experience may be more appropriate. Charges for services rendered in connection with such matters will be billed at the Discounted Hourly Rate. (In the case of lawyers other than project team members, the Discounted Hourly Rate will be a reduced hourly rate proportionately comparable to the discounts reflected on the attached Exhibit A.)

Assumptions on Which This Proposal Is Based

The proposal we have set forth rests on several assumptions. These assumptions reflect our collective experience with alternative fee structures. The pertinent assumptions are as follows:

1. The quoted structures are based on our mutual agreement that [law firm] will represent the Client throughout the Project's development. The fee structures we have outlined depend on our having confidence that our project team will be able to devote significant time to Project matters.

2. The quoted structures also depend on our ability to work together to lay the groundwork for the Client's systematic representation. Specifically, we believe that cost-effective representation in developing the Project will require (i) that we have a regular chance to review sales and leasing strategy with the Client and to assemble some objective guidance to direct us as we go forward, and (ii) that we work together with the Client—and with any brokers involved on the Client's behalf—to establish a uniform approach to the contemplated sales and leasing transactions. We should work together, for example, to establish objective criteria on some of the most important legal and business points (cost pass-throughs, indemnities, and environmental provisions, for example) that we will face in every sale and lease transaction. As for point (ii), our experience recommends that we spend some time putting together a form of term sheet that proactively seeks to resolve key legal and business points in every deal even before lawyers become involved.

3. We must have regular, personal contact with you and your business people. Communication is important; personal contact and personal relationships help cultivate good communication. Accordingly, we should commit ourselves together at the outset to regular, face-to-face meetings with a specified core of Project team members.

4. Availability of individual lawyers will occasionally require that we staff matters with other firm members of comparable experience and repute. From time to time, circumstances will dictate that a Project team member be unavailable. In these unusual instances, we may—subject to your approving our selection—temporarily substitute another firm member of comparable experience and repute. If the particular matter is subject to billing on a Fixed Fee or Unit Fee basis, the substitution will not affect the total fee. If the particular matter is subject to billing on a Discounted Hourly Fee or Maximum Fee basis, the services of the replacement lawyer will be billed at a reduced hourly rate proportionately comparable to the discounts reflected on the attached <u>Exhibit A</u>. In no instance will a substitution affect the specified fee cap under a Maximum Fee.

5. No matter what the governing fee structure, statements of account will include an additional charge for disbursements made for photocopying, outgoing telecopies, local and overnight delivery charges, travel outside Grace County, and charges for computerized legal research on outside databases for which we are charged access fees. We constantly strive to keep these charges at or below market rates. The Client will not be billed for a number of other items that, in our experience, other law firms routinely charge for—including library serv-

ices, administrative computer time, domestic long-distance telephone calls, ordinary postage, secretarial straight time, or equipment overhead.

Some Final Thoughts on Risk

Finally, experience has taught us that our efforts in transactional matters like this depend in large part on the tendencies and negotiating posture of our Client. The rates quoted in this proposal are based on data from many different transactions we have handled, as well as on the contact we have had with the Client over the past several months. Nonetheless, unforeseen situations will arise.

We expect to assume the risk of many of these situations. If truly unusual circumstances were to arise, though, we would notify you of those circumstances in writing as soon as possible, and would then trust that such instances would be handled in good faith and in a spirit of fairness both by the Client and by [law firm].

Exhibit A
Project Team Hourly Services Rates

Team Member	Standard Hourly Rate	Discounted Hourly Rate
Adams		
Brown		
Carter		
Davis		
Ellis		
Fox		
Legal Assistant		

NOTE: Hourly services rates are subject to change annually as of _____.

Index

Note: Information presented in figures is indicated by *f*.

Selected Books from . . .
THE ABA LAW PRACTICE MANAGEMENT SECTION

**How to Draft Bills Clients Rush to Pay,
Second Edition**
By J. Harris Morgan and Jay G Foonberg
Spend an hour or two with noted law practice management authorities Morgan and Foonberg as they take
you step by step through the process of building the
client relationship, setting the appropriate fee agreement, and drafting the bill that will get you paid. You'll
find, in plain language, a rational and workable
approach to creating fee agreements and bills that satisfy your clients, build their trust, and motivate them
to pay. Comparisons and samples of fee agreements
and invoices are integrated throughout the text, along
with a clear explanation of which methods work best—
and why.

**Paralegals, Profitability, and the
Future of Your Law Practice**
By Arthur G. Greene and Therese A. Cannon
Effectively integrate paralegals into your practice, and
expand their roles to ensure your firm is successful in
the next decade with this essential resource. If you're
not currently using paralegals, you'll learn why you
need them and how to create and implement a successful paralegal model in your practice. If you're
already using paralegals, you'll learn how to ensure
your paralegal program is structured properly, runs
effectively, and continually contributes to your bottom
line. Valuable appendices contain sample job descriptions, model guidelines, confidentiality agreements,
performance evaluations, and other useful resources,
also provided on the accompanying CD-ROM for ease
in implementation!

**Results-Oriented Financial Management:
A Step-By-Step Guide to Law Firm Profitability,
Second Edition**
By John G. Iezzi, CPA
This hands-on, how-to book will assist managing partners, law firm managers, and law firm accountants by
providing them with the budgeting and financial knowledge they need to need to make the critical decisions.
Whether you're a financial novice or veteran manager,
this book will help you examine every facet of your
financial affairs from cash flow and budget creation to
billing and compensation. Also included with the book
are valuable financial models on CD-ROM allowing you
to compute profitability and determine budgets by
inputting your own data. The appendix contains useful
forms and examples from lawyers who have actually
implemented alternative billing methods at their firms.

**Collecting Your Fee:
Getting Paid From Intake to Invoice**.
By Edward Poll
This practical and user-friendly guide provides you
with proven strategies and sound advice that will
make the process of collecting your fees simpler, easier, and more effective! This handy resource provides
you with the framework around which to structure
your collection efforts. You'll learn how you can
streamline your billing and collection process by hiring the appropriate staff, establishing strong client
relationships from the start, and issuing client-friendly
invoices. In addition, you'll benefit from the strategies
to use when the client fails to pay the bill on time and
what you need to do to get paid when all else fails.
Also included is a CD-ROM with sample forms, letters,
agreements, and more for you to customize to your
own practice needs.

**The Lawyer's Guide to Adobe® Acrobat®,
Third Edition**
By David L. Masters
This book was written to help lawyers increase
productivity, decrease costs, and improve client
services by moving from paper-based files to digital
records. This updated and revised edition focuses
on the ways lawyers can benefit from using the most
current software, Adobe® Acrobat® 8, to create
Portable Document Format (PDF) files. The latest
version of Acrobat has a number of useful features
for the legal professional, including Bates numbering
and redaction.

**Risk Management: Survival Tools for Law Firms,
Second Edition**
By Anthony E. Davis and Peter R. Jarvis
This book helps your firm establish solid policies,
procedures, and systems to minimize risk. This com-
pletely revised edition and accompanying CD provides a comprehensive overview of risk management,
offers a practical approach to risk management evaluation, and steps to take to create a "best practice"
plan. Using a practical self-audit tool, the book enables lawyers to consider how well their firms are
addressing each of the key components of effective
risk management.

ABA **LawPracticeManagementSection**
MARKETING • MANAGEMENT • TECHNOLOGY • FINANCE

The Essential Formbook:
Comprehensive Management Tools for Lawyers
Volume I: Partnership and Organizational
Agreements/Client Intake and Fee Agreements
Volume II: Human Resources/
Fees, Billing, and Collection
Volume III: Calendar and File Management/
Law Firm Financial Analysis
Volume IV: Disaster Planning and Recovery/
Risk Management and Professional Liability Insurance
By Gary A. Munneke and Anthony E. Davis
Useful to legal practitioners of all specialties and sizes, these volumes will help you establish profitable, affirmative client relationships so you can avoid unnecessary risks associated with malpractice and disciplinary complaints. And, with all the forms available on CD-ROM, it's easy to modify them to match your specific needs. Visit our Web site at www.lawpractice.org/catalog/511-0424 for more information about this invaluable resource.

The Lawyer's Guide to Strategic Planning:
Defining, Setting, and Achieving Your Firm's Goals
By Thomas C. Grella and Michael L. Hudkins
This practice-building resource is your guide to planning dynamic strategic plans and implementing them at your firm. You'll learn about the actual planning process and how to establish goals in key planning areas such as law firm governance, competition, opening a new office, financial management, technology, marketing and competitive intelligence, client development and retention, and more. The accompanying CD-ROM contains a wealth of policies, statements, and other sample documents. If you're serious about improving the way your firm works, increasing productivity, making better decisions, and setting your firm on the right course—this is the resource you need.

Anatomy of a Law Firm Merger:
How to Make or Break the Deal,
Third Edition
By Hildebrandt International
How can you effectively navigate the merger process? This updated Third Edition can help you decide when to consider a merger and how to make the many other decisions involved in completing the merger and ultimately integrating the merged firm. This resource will help you to consider the right and wrong reasons to merge, analyze strengths and weaknesses, and formulate specific goals for the merger. The book also contains valuable exhibits, questionnaires, and checklists—furnished in text and CD-ROM formats.

Unbundling Legal Services:
A Guide to Delivering Legal Services a la Carte
By Forrest S. Mosten
Unbundling, the practice of supplying the client discrete lawyering tasks according to the client's direction, is changing the face of the legal profession today. Given minor modifications, any firm can start unbundling their law practice and offer this new consumer-oriented approach to legal service delivery to their clients. Learn how to set up and manage an unbundling law practice, get new clients, and market this new area of your practice. Offered as a supplement to a traditional full-service practice, you will recapture market share and gain professional satisfaction by offering this innovative service.

The ABA Guide to Lawyer Trust Accounts
By Jay G Foonberg
Avoid the pitfalls of trust account rules violations! Designed as a self-study course or as seminar materials, with short, stand-alone chapters that walk you through the procedures of client trust accounting. This indispensable reference outlines the history of applicable ethics rules; how you could inadvertently be violating those rules; ways to work with your banker and accountant to set up the office systems you need; numerous forms that you can adapt for your office (including self-tests for seminars and CLE credits); plus Foonberg's "10 rules of good trust account procedures" and "10 steps to good trust account records"—intended to work with whatever local rules your state mandates.

The Lawyer's Guide to Marketing Your Practice,
Second Edition
Edited by James A. Durham and Deborah McMurray
This book is packed with practical ideas, innovative strategies, useful checklists, and sample marketing and action plans to help you implement a successful, multifaceted, and profit-enhancing marketing plan for your firm. Organized into four sections, this illuminating resource covers: Developing Your Approach; Enhancing Your Image; Implementing Marketing Strategies and Maintaining Your Program. Appendix materials include an instructive primer on market research to inform you on research methodologies that support the marketing of legal services. The accompanying CD-ROM contains a wealth of checklists, plans, and other sample reports, questionnaires, and templates—all designed to make implementing your marketing strategy as easy as possible.

30-Day Risk-Free Order Form
Call Today! 1-800-285-2221
Monday–Friday, 7:30 AM – 5:30 PM, Central Time

Qty	Title	LPM Price	Regular Price	Total
_____	ABA Guide to Lawyer Trust Accounts (5110374)	$ 69.95	$ 79.95	$_____
_____	Anatomy of a Law Firm Merger, Third Edition (5110506)	79.95	94.95	$_____
_____	Collecting Your Fee: Getting Paid From Intake to Invoice (5110490)	69.95	79.95	$_____
_____	The Essential Formbook, Volume I (5110424V1)	169.95	199.95	$_____
_____	The Essential Formbook, Volume II (5110424V2)	169.95	199.95	$_____
_____	The Essential Formbook, Volume III (5110424V3)	169.95	199.95	$_____
_____	The Essential Formbook, Volume IV (5110424V4)	169.95	199.95	$_____
_____	How to Draft Bills Clients Rush to Pay, Second Edition (5110495)	57.95	67.95	$_____
_____	The Lawyer's Guide to Adobe Acrobat, Third Edition (5110588)	49.95	79.95	$_____
_____	The Lawyer's Guide to Marketing Your Practice, Second Edition (5110500)	79.95	89.95	$_____
_____	The Lawyer's Guide to Strategic Planning (5110520)	59.95	79.95	$_____
_____	Paralegals, Profitability, and the Future of Your Law Practice (5110491)	59.95	69.95	$_____
_____	Results-Oriented Financial Management, Second Edition (5110493)	89.95	99.95	$_____
_____	Unbundling Legal Services (5110448)	54.95	64.95	$_____
_____	Risk Management: Survival Tools for Law Firms, Second Edition (5110653)	79.95	89.95	$_____

*Postage and Handling	
$10.00 to $24.99	$5.95
$25.00 to $49.99	$9.95
$50.00 to $99.99	$12.95
$100.00 to $349.99	$17.95
$350 to $499.99	$24.95

**Tax
DC residents add 5.75%
IL residents add 9.00%

*Postage and Handling	$_____
**Tax	$_____
TOTAL	$_____

PAYMENT

❏ Check enclosed (to the ABA)

❏ Visa   ❏ MasterCard   ❏ American Express

Account Number   Exp. Date   Signature

Name _____ Firm _____

Address _____

City _____ State _____ Zip _____

Phone Number _____ E-Mail Address _____

Note: E-Mail address is required if ordering the
The Lawyer's Guide to Fact Finding on the Internet
E-mail Newsletter (5110498)

Guarantee
If—for any reason—you are not satisfied with your purchase, you may
return it within 30 days of receipt for a complete refund of the price of the
book(s). No questions asked!

Mail: ABA Publication Orders, P.O. Box 10892, Chicago, Illinois 60610-0892
♦ Phone: 1-800-285-2221 ♦ FAX: 312-988-5568

E-Mail: abasvcctr@abanet.org ♦ Internet: http://www.lawpractice.org/catalog

Are You in Your Element?

Tap into the Resources of the ABA Law Practice Management Section

ABA Law Practice Management Section Membership Benefits

The ABA Law Practice Management Section (LPM) is a professional membership organization of the American Bar Association that helps lawyers and other legal professionals with the business of practicing law. LPM focuses on providing information and resources in the core areas of marketing, management, technology, and finance through its award-winning magazine, teleconference series, Webzine, educational programs (CLE), Web site, and publishing division. For more than thirty years, LPM has established itself as a leader within the ABA and the profession-at-large by producing the world's largest legal technology conference (ABA TECHSHOW®) each year. In addition, LPM's publishing program is one of the largest in the ABA, with more than eighty-five titles in print.

In addition to significant book discounts, LPM Section membership offers these benefits:

ABA TECHSHOW
Membership includes a $100 discount to ABA TECHSHOW, the world's largest legal technology conference & expo!

Teleconference Series
Convenient, monthly CLE teleconferences on hot topics in marketing, management, technology and finance. Access educational opportunities from the comfort of your office chair – today's practical way to earn CLE credits!

Law Practice Magazine
Eight issues of our award-winning *Law Practice* magazine, full of insightful articles and practical tips on Marketing/Client Development, Practice Management, Legal Technology, and Finance.

Law Practice Today
LPM's unique Web-based magazine covers all the hot topics in law practice management today — identify current issues, face today's challenges, find solutions quickly. Visit www.lawpracticetoday.org.

Law Technology Today
LPM's newest Webzine focuses on legal technology issues in law practice management — covering a broad spectrum of the technology, tools, strategies and their implementation to help lawyers build a successful practice. Visit www.lawtechnologytoday.org.

LawPractice.news
Brings Section news, educational opportunities, book releases, and special offers to members via e-mail each month.

To learn more about the ABA Law Practice Management Section, visit www.lawpractice.org or call 1-800-285-2221.

MARKETING • MANAGEMENT • TECHNOLOGY • FINANCE

About the CD

The accompanying CD contains the text of the Appendices from *Winning Alternatives to the Billable Hour*, Third Edition. The files are in Microsoft Word® format.

For additional information about the files on the CD, please open and read the **"readme.doc"** file on the CD.

NOTE: The set of files on the CD may only be used on a single computer or moved to and used on another computer. Under no circumstances may the set of files be used on more than one computer at one time. If you are interested in obtaining a license to use the set of files on a local network, please contact: Director, Copyrights and Contracts, American Bar Association, 321 N. Clark Street, Chicago, IL 60654, (312) 988-6101. **Please read the license and warranty statements on the following page before using this CD.**

Defending Liberty Pursuing Justice

CD-ROM to accompany
Winning Alternatives to the Billable Hour, Third Edition

WARNING: Opening this package indicates your understanding and acceptance of the following Terms and Conditions.

READ THE FOLLOWING TERMS AND CONDITIONS BEFORE OPENING THIS SEALED PACKAGE. IF YOU DO NOT AGREE WITH THEM, PROMPTLY RETURN THE UNOPENED PACKAGE TO EITHER THE PARTY FROM WHOM IT WAS ACQUIRED OR TO THE AMERICAN BAR ASSOCIATION AND YOUR MONEY WILL BE RETURNED.

The document files in this package are a proprietary product of the American Bar Association and are protected by Copyright Law. The American Bar Association retains title to and ownership of these files.

License

You may use this set of files on a single computer or move it to and use it on another computer, but under no circumstances may you use the set of files on more than one computer at the same time. You may copy the files either in support of your use of the files on a single computer or for backup purposes. If you are interested in obtaining a license to use the set of files on a local network, please contact: Manager, Publication Policies & Contracting, American Bar Association, 321 N. Clark Street, Chicago, IL 60654, (312) 988-6101.

You may permanently transfer the set of files to another party if the other party agrees to accept the terms and conditions of this License Agreement. If you transfer the set of files, you must at the same time transfer all copies of the files to the same party or destroy those not transferred. Such transfer terminates your license. You may not rent, lease, assign or otherwise transfer the files except as stated in this paragraph.

You may modify these files for your own use within the provisions of this License Agreement. You may not redistribute any modified files.

Warranty

If a CD-ROM in this package is defective, the American Bar Association will replace it at no charge if the defective diskette is returned to the American Bar Association within 60 days from the date of acquisition.

American Bar Association warrants that these files will perform in substantial compliance with the documentation supplied in this package. However, the American Bar Association does not warrant these forms as to the correctness of the legal material contained therein. If you report a significant defect in performance in writing to the American Bar Association, and the American Bar Association is not able to correct it within 60 days, you may return the CD, including all copies and documentation, to the American Bar Association and the American Bar Association will refund your money.

Any files that you modify will no longer be covered under this warranty even if they were modified in accordance with the License Agreement and product documentation.

IN NO EVENT WILL THE AMERICAN BAR ASSOCIATION, ITS OFFICERS, MEMBERS, OR EMPLOYEES BE LIABLE TO YOU FOR ANY DAMAGES, INCLUDING LOST PROFITS, LOST SAVINGS OR OTHER INCIDENTAL OR CONSEQUENTIAL DAMAGES ARISING OUT OF YOUR USE OR INABILITY TO USE THESE FILES EVEN IF THE AMERICAN BAR ASSOCIATION OR AN AUTHORIZED AMERICAN BAR ASSOCIATION REPRESENTATIVE HAS BEEN ADVISED OF THE POSSIBILITY OF SUCH DAMAGES, OR FOR ANY CLAIM BY ANY OTHER PARTY. SOME STATES DO NOT ALLOW THE LIMITATION OR EXCLUSION OF LIABILITY FOR INCIDENTAL OR CONSEQUENTIAL DAMAGES, IN WHICH CASE THIS LIMITATION MAY NOT APPLY TO YOU.